STRESS-FREE LEADERSHIP

Fantasy or Reality

ABDUL HAFIDZ WIN

notionpress.com

INDIA · SINGAPORE · MALAYSIA

CONTENTS

INTRODUCTION

Leadership often feels like pushing a boulder uphill. There's never a moment to rest, and the effort never truly ends. The journey never stops. The stakes are always high. Stress turns into a relentless presence, influencing choices and diminishing concentration. For numerous individuals, the concept of leading without stress seems like a dream. Can one truly lead without feeling overwhelmed? Is it possible for leaders to effectively manage their duties while remaining composed and attentive? These are the inquiries that this book examines. *Stress-Free Leadership: Reality or Fantasy?* not only questions the feasibility of stress-free leadership. It demonstrates how leaders can organize their thinking, strategies, and approaches to make them achievable.

The title questions a widely held belief. Many consider stress-free leadership to be a myth, an appealing concept that fails in reality. Leadership involves difficult choices, extended hours, and ongoing troubleshooting. But must stress characterize the journey? This book investigates further. Is it truly a fantasy, or is it something that leaders can intentionally bring about? The objective here isn't flawlessness. It's not about acting like stress isn't real. It's about handling stress in ways that enable leaders to flourish.

How do you move forward without being held back by stress? It starts with a fresh perspective. Stress isn't just a burden. It's a signal. It shows where your leadership style might need attention. Ignoring stress or pushing through without reflection doesn't solve the problem. Stress lingers. It grows, affecting energy, focus, and relationships. The first step to stress-free leadership is recognizing that pattern and deciding to break it.

Think about your own leadership journey. How often have you really considered how you deal with stress? Is it something you simply accept, or do you see it as something you can manage? Most leaders get caught reacting to stress instead of addressing the causes. They try to outwork it, pushing harder and hoping the pressure will ease. But this approach rarely works. It drains energy, leaves teams struggling, and pushes burnout to the forefront.

Here's the good news. The cycle of stress can be broken. Stress-free leadership doesn't mean you'll never face challenges. It's about finding ways to manage them without losing control. It's about understanding what triggers your stress and knowing how to respond. It's about creating habits that make stress less overwhelming. Most importantly, it's about finding balance, not perfection, so you can lead with focus and purpose.

This journey begins with a single thought. Being a leader doesn't mean sacrificing your well-being. You can change your strategy. You can implement strategies that generate consistent momentum in your leadership while avoiding being overwhelmed by stress. It is feasible to guide in a manner that seems both efficient and controllable.

In the upcoming chapters, we will approach this gradually. Initially, we'll examine ways to generate momentum in your leadership while managing stress effectively. This implies grasping what restricts you and how to progress with clear insight. Next, we'll examine why leaders must reconsider their approach to managing stress. Stress is not merely a hurdle to conquer. It's something you can collaborate with.

Ultimately, we will respond to the inquiry presented in the title. Is leadership without stress a reality or simply a fantasy? The reality is, it's not either. It's a perspective, a collection of choices, and a manner of guiding that is completely attainable for you.

The Purpose Behind This Book

Leadership is not an easy path. It challenges you in ways that test your focus, patience, and ability to adapt. Stress often feels like a constant shadow, shaping every decision you make. This book was created to offer a fresh perspective. Its purpose is clear. It's about giving you practical strategies that you can apply right away, helping you stay effective no matter how difficult things get, and showing you how to create balance so stress doesn't control every part of your life.

Let's start with the first reason. You need tools you can actually use. Theory is fine, but without action, it doesn't help when things get tough. Think about the last time stress overwhelmed you. Maybe your to-do list was endless, or a problem came out of nowhere and disrupted your plans. What did you do? Most leaders try to push through, hoping to stay ahead. But that approach can create more frustration. This book offers something different. It gives you steps you can take right now to ease the pressure. For example, when a task feels too big, breaking it into smaller steps can make it feel less intimidating. Learning to take quick pauses during a chaotic day can give you the space to reset. These strategies aren't complicated. They're small shifts that make a big difference.

The second purpose is to keep you effective. Stress doesn't just wear you out physically. It clouds your mind. It can make you doubt your decisions or react without thinking. Have you ever faced a situation where the pressure was so high you couldn't focus? Stress affects your ability to lead clearly. This book helps you recognize that. It's not about pretending stress doesn't exist. It's about stopping it from taking over. When you manage stress, you show up differently. You think clearly, make better decisions, and communicate in ways that build trust. Your ability to lead improves because you are working from a calmer, more focused place.

The third reason is balance. Stress doesn't remain confined to a single area. It can affect your job, your residence, your well-being, and your connections. It influences your communication style with your team and the connections you maintain with those you value. That's the reason balance is important. However, balance does not imply doing less. It involves handling your time and energy to allow for rest, recuperation, and activities that bring you happiness. By looking after yourself, you become more effective at caring for others. This book motivates you to develop habits that allow you to lead while maintaining your sense of balance. It's not about evading difficulties. It's about managing them in a manner that suits you.

Why concentrate on these three concepts? Stress doesn't need to be the main motivating factor in your leadership path. The tactics and strategies in this book aren't meant to burden you with additional responsibilities. They're here to assist you in handling your duties in a manner that seems manageable. They assist you in leading with increased energy and clarity. Every chapter will expand on these concepts, leading you progressively to a fresh approach to thinking and doing.

Let's move forward. Whatever we discuss here will bring you closer to leading with less stress and more purpose.

Personal Lessons and Experiences That Shaped This Book

This book was not born out of theory. It came from years of my real-life experiences, moments of pressure, reflection, and growth. Over three decades of working across industries, running businesses, and leading teams have taught me lessons that no classroom could offer. These are the insights I bring to you, built through trials, challenges, and a constant desire to learn.

One of my earliest lessons came from my time at KPMG as an auditor. It was a role that demanded precision and composure under pressure. Deadlines were tight. Expectations were high. In that fast-paced environment,

I quickly learned how to manage stress without letting it compromise the quality of my work. Staying calm when numbers didn't add up or when the clock was ticking became second nature. Those moments taught me that stress can be addressed, not ignored.

After KPMG, I moved into the corporate world, taking on roles as an accountant, finance manager, and executive director in both private and public-listed companies. This experience gave me direct exposure to the workings of the corporate environment, from mid-level management to high-level decision-making. The pressure during corporate exercises, such as listing a company on the stock exchange, mergers and acquisitions, and fund-raising activities, was immense. These processes required complete dedication, long hours, and the ability to juggle multiple responsibilities at once. The demands of coordinating with various government agencies, financial institutions, and internal departments pushed me to manage stress effectively. At just 26 years old, I had already climbed to the corporate level, handling responsibilities that carried significant weight while many of my peers were still in junior positions. The early exposure to high-stakes decision-making taught me resilience, adaptability, and the importance of staying composed under pressure.

From there, I moved into the world of entrepreneurship, running an ICT-related business. Leading my own company brought a new kind of stress. I was no longer just an employee. I was responsible for the company's future, my team's growth, and keeping clients happy. Problems often came out of nowhere. Technology fails. Teams miscommunicate. I learned the importance of staying adaptable, thinking on my feet, and building trust with the people around me.

Working in Malaysia and dealing with various international business organizations exposed me to international businesses and multicultural teams. Every person brought a different perspective, and every culture shaped how challenges were approached. These experiences taught me how to connect with people from all walks of life. Leading in this environment required both firm decision-making and an understanding of what people needed to succeed. Leadership is never just about systems, it's about people.

My roles as CFO, CEO, and public-listed director of medium-sized companies brought an added weight of responsibility. I was accountable not just to teams but to shareholders, clients, and the public. Leading during difficult times, when decisions felt heavier than ever, taught me the importance of balance. I needed to make tough calls, but I also needed to listen, empathize, and keep morale strong. It was a constant balancing act, and it showed me that leadership without emotional awareness leads to burnout for yourself and those around you.

Outside of my professional life, my experiences have been just as valuable. Owning and managing a professional badminton club introduced me to a different kind of leadership. Sports demand discipline, teamwork, and resilience. Watching players push through setbacks on the court reminded me that leadership is not about avoiding challenges but staying focused despite them. It's the same principle I carried into running an antique gallery and a traditional eco-tourism resort. Both ventures brought unexpected obstacles, but they also brought joy. They reminded me of the importance of stepping away, finding balance, and reconnecting with what energizes you.

Travel has also been one of my greatest teachers. Visiting over 20 countries from various continents gave me a deeper understanding of leadership cultures beyond borders. Each culture provided a new way of thinking about stress, communication and growth. I saw leaders who led with patience, teams who worked with quiet determination, and environments where simplicity brought clarity. Those lessons have stayed with me. They have shaped the way I see leadership as something both universal and deeply personal.

The combination of my work as a Chartered Accountant, businessman, and leader has taught me that stress is not the enemy. It's a challenge to manage. Whether I was leading teams in corporate offices, overseeing professional athletes, or handling the complexities of small businesses, the principles remained the same. Balance, clarity, and self-awareness matter. You cannot control every challenge that comes your way, but you can control how you respond to it.

Through every step of my journey, I've learned that leadership is not about being perfect. It's about being present. It's about finding practical ways to stay grounded when the demands feel overwhelming. This book comes from those lessons. It's here to offer and share strategies you can use, real tools that have worked in my life and can possibly work in your environment, too.

The purpose of sharing these experiences is not to tell you what to do. It's to let you know that stress can be managed and leadership can be balanced. With the right mindset, you can lead effectively without sacrificing your energy, focus, or well-being. Let's keep moving forward as we continue exploring what it means to lead with purpose and clarity.

01

THE TRUTH ABOUT STRESS-FREE LEADERSHIP

Leadership is frequently discussed regarding accomplishments and significant milestones. Yet underneath, there is an unseen battle that often does not receive sufficient focus. Stress may seem like an unavoidable aspect of leadership. It tracks leaders during meetings, choices, and all intense situations. This chapter poses a challenging question: Is it truly feasible to lead without stress, or are we merely inviting disappointment by pursuing an unrealistic goal?

To address that, we must sincerely examine what stress-free leadership truly signifies and why it appears so unattainable. Leadership involves ongoing expectations. The demand to succeed, the obligation to lead others, and the unforeseen obstacles, it all accumulates. Is the burden leaders bear an immutable truth, or can it be managed in another way?

This section examines two main concepts. Initially, we will explore why the idea of stress-free leadership appears unattainable for numerous individuals. Next, we will reveal the everyday challenges leaders encounter and how these challenges affect not just their efficiency but also their mental and emotional health.

1.1 The Idea of Stress-Free Leadership and Why It Feels Unattainable

Leadership without stress seems to be the perfect approach to guiding others. Who wouldn't desire to tackle each challenge with assurance, staying concentrated without becoming stressed? However, for many leaders, this concept seems difficult to achieve. Leadership naturally presents challenges that appear linked to stress, pressing deadlines, difficult choices, and ongoing expectations. The idea of leading without pressure often seems more like a fantasy to most leaders rather than an achievable goal through proper stress management.

What makes stress-free leadership seem unreachable for the majority of leaders? One reason stems from the expectations imposed on them. Leaders are frequently viewed as solution-finders who are expected to possess all the answers. They are anticipated to manage crises smoothly, make choices in stressful situations, and lead their teams confidently. These unachievable expectations impose a significant weight, causing leaders to feel they cannot acknowledge their difficulties. The demand to seem tough and steadfast can occasionally be more taxing than the challenges themselves.

Plans seldom unfold as anticipated. Abrupt market fluctuations, unforeseen team obstacles, and changing priorities necessitate continual adjustment. For numerous leaders, this uncertainty strengthens the conviction that stress is an inescapable aspect of the role. They become trapped in a loop of responding to issues rather than confronting the underlying causes of stress.

In addition to external factors, internal pressures also play a role in the challenge. Numerous leaders set unrealistically high expectations for themselves, convinced they need to excel in all areas. This self-inflicted pressure frequently heightens feelings of stress. They exert themselves to work more intensely, assume additional duties, and make trade-offs to achieve their objectives, all while disregarding the impact on their health.

The reality is that stress-free leadership doesn't involve removing obstacles or being resistant to stress. It's about rethinking the definition of success. Rather than seeking perfection, leaders should concentrate on developing resilience and learning to handle stress in a manner that keeps them effective. This entails seeing stress as an indication rather than a setback. It indicates that an issue requires focus, be it workload, priorities, or individual habits.

By shifting the focus from avoiding stress to controlling its impact, leaders can move closer to a balanced approach. Stress-free leadership doesn't mean never feeling pressure. It means understanding how to respond to it in ways that protect your energy, enhance your focus, and support your goals.

This shift isn't easy, but it's possible. Leaders who learn to manage stress as a part of their journey rather than as an enemy to fight can find new ways to thrive. It's not about erasing stress. It's about changing the role it plays in your leadership.

1.2 The Realities of the Pressure Leaders Face Every Day

Recognizing that stress-free leadership entails managing rather than eliminating stress is an essential first step. However, even when leaders change their viewpoint, the pressures of everyday realities persist. These stresses are persistent, diverse, and frequently unyielding. To genuinely understand what stress-free leadership entails in reality, we need to examine the challenges that leaders encounter daily and how those challenges lead to a cycle of stress.

Stress is not a rare visitor in a leader's life. It's constantly around. Every day presents a unique blend of difficulties. Deadlines become stricter, priorities change, and unforeseen problems arise. Leadership frequently resembles balancing multiple tasks while on unstable terrain. Each choice, regardless of its size, seems important. The burden of these choices can be draining, and the stress continues even after the workday is over.

The demands imposed on leaders intensify this pressure. Leaders are not only required to function but to surpass expectations. Their choices are examined closely, and their errors are amplified. Have you ever experienced the burden of everyone relying on you? It's an ongoing fact for many leaders. They are anticipated to stay calm, offer guidance, and achieve outcomes, regardless of how difficult the circumstances are.

However, external pressures represent only one aspect of the issue. Expectations from within can be even more burdensome. Numerous leaders impose unrealistically elevated expectations on themselves. They believe they are accountable for results that are well outside their influence. This pressure created by oneself frequently results in extended working hours, increased responsibilities, and compromising personal health to achieve their objectives. The conviction that they need to manage everything flawlessly introduces an additional level of stress.

Leading also involves overseeing relationships. It's not solely about directing teams or establishing objectives. It's about managing disagreements, assisting individuals, and building trust. Misunderstandings, conflicts in personality, or unfulfilled expectations can render these interactions tense. Leaders frequently believe they need to take on the tension to ensure the team progresses. However, shouldering that emotional weight without an outlet can negatively affect you over time.

The stress isn't confined to the workplace. It permeates personal life. Leaders frequently find themselves pondering work long after the day has ended. Stress manifests in their relations with family and friends, in sleepless nights, and in a persistent feeling of extreme tiredness resulting from mental or physical stress. If not addressed, it can affect physical health, emotional stability, and even the relationships that leaders value the most.

Despite these pressures, many leaders hesitate to acknowledge the toll stress takes on them. They worry that admitting their struggles will make them seem weak or less capable. However, recognizing stress is not a failure. It's the first step to handling it in a way that doesn't harm them or those around them.

The reality is that leadership will always come with challenges. The question isn't whether you will face pressure. It's how you choose to handle it. When you understand the demands of leadership and the stress they bring, you're better equipped to create strategies that protect your well-being while maintaining your effectiveness.

1.3 Is it something we can truly achieve, or are we setting ourselves up for disappointment?

Stress-free leadership is an appealing concept., but is it achievable? Numerous leaders wonder if it's achievable or if the quest itself is leading them toward frustration due to high expectations. These concerns are legitimate and valid in the corporate world and day-to-day life. Leadership frequently involve in unlimited and complex series of requests, leaving minimal opportunity for contemplation and reflection.

To address this question, it is essential to rephrase what stress-free leadership signifies. It's not about completely removing stress. Stress is a normal reaction to accountability, and leadership is abundant in it. Rather, the aim is to establish a controllable relationship with stress. This involves creating habits and systems that minimize its intensity and stop it from dominating.

When leaders view stress-free leadership as an absolute objective, disappointment is nearly certain. The notion of never experiencing stress is unrealistic. Obstacles will emerge and deadlines will approach. Conflicts will require quick resolution in running a business. The essential point is not to remove these truths but to react to them in a different way. Leaders who view stress as an obstacle to overcome instead of something to evade can foster enduring changes in their approach to their responsibilities.

Consider how minor changes can lead to significant impacts in our decision or strategies. Establishing limits on your time, assigning duties to reliable team members, or prioritizing tasks can minimize unnecessary stress. These are actionable measures that don't necessitate a total transformation of your leadership approach. They just need a readiness to abandon the notion that you must accomplish everything flawlessly.

It's also essential to redefine what success entails. Success isn't about accomplishing everything. It's about prioritizing what is most important. Leaders frequently think that leading without stress involves managing every detail of their responsibilities and their teams. This mindset fosters a loop of micromanagement and excessive commitments, which merely increases our stress level. Instead, the leader should reflect on what really matters for them to focus and avoid unnecessary stress. Are you directing your time and effort toward activities that correspond with your objectives? Do you have faith that your team will manage their responsibilities? When leaders concentrate on what is important, they liberate themselves from extra loads.

Another essential aspect of achieving stress-free leadership is embracing imperfection. Leadership lacks a manual, and no leader possesses all the solutions. Errors occur and not all plans succeed as what we wanted. When leaders accept this reality, they cease viewing every obstacle as a personal shortcoming. This change enables them to progress with assurance, even when encountering obstacles.

Leadership without stress also involves fostering resilience. Resilient leaders do not shy away from stress, they adjust to it. They identify when stress is increasing and take proactive measures to handle it. This could entail taking a moment to consider the source of stress, consulting with reliable coworkers, or merely stepping away to rejuvenate. Resilience does not pertain to strength. It's about adaptability, the capacity to flex without shattering.

Leaders should also take into account how their mindset influences outcomes. If you perceive stress as an unbeatable barrier, it will seem unmanageable. However, viewing it as a challenge to conquer makes it easier to handle. This does not imply overlooking the truths of stress. It signifies tackling it with the awareness that you possess the skills and resources to manage it. When leaders foster this attitude, they create a basis for enduring achievement in their careers.

It's important to consider: Is stress-free leadership focused on you, or is it about the role model you provide for others? Leaders who master stress management effectively motivate their teams to follow suit. They encourage atmospheres where a peaceful working environment and concentration are prioritized over perpetual haste. This ripple effect reduces stress not only for the leader but for the whole team as well.

In the end, attaining stress-free leadership isn't about establishing an ideal work atmosphere or evading difficulties. It's about developing habits that enable you to manage stress in a manner that fosters your objectives and well-being. Advancement is more important than flawlessness. Every tiny step, be it mastering delegation, focusing on self-care, or changing your perspective on setbacks, moves you nearer to a more sustainable leadership style.

This leads us to the subsequent challenge. In the current digital landscape, the challenges that leaders encounter are heightened. Technology has transformed our work environment, as well as the ways we encounter stress. Let's examine effective ways to tackle these contemporary issues.

1.4 Managing Stress in the Digital Era

The digital era has changed how we live and work. It has linked teams across the globe, accelerated communication, and introduced new resources to address issues quicker than ever. However, along with these advancements arise fresh challenges. For numerous leaders, the digital age presents a double-edged challenge in running day-to-day business. Although technology has simplified certain aspects of work, it has also heightened the demand to deliver results, react swiftly and remain constantly connected.

Picture a leader managing a team dispersed over various time zones and locations. Their day begins early with emails and messages from one area and concludes late with updates from another. Alerts appear continuously, diverting their focus in multiple directions. Meetings coincide, and responsibilities accumulate. The task continues even after several hours. A notification on their phone might indicate an urgent matter requiring attention. This is a common situation. It's the truth about leadership in an ever-connected digital world.

A major challenge of the digital age is the demand for uninterrupted accessibility. Emails, instant messages, and alerts disregard boundaries. They come at any time, generating a feeling of urgency that can be difficult to overlook. Leaders experience the urgency to react quickly, worried that any delays could be interpreted as ineffectiveness or a lack of dedication. With time, this constant connectivity diminishes their ability to concentrate, rejuvenate, and maintain a balanced approach to managing daily tasks.

To handle stress in the digital age, leaders must oversee their interactions with technology. The initial step involves establishing limits. For instance, disabling notifications outside of work hours can aid in establishing a distinction between professional and personal life. Leaders can likewise set designated times for reviewing emails or replying to messages. By establishing clear expectations with their teams, they can promote a healthier work culture in which everyone honors these limits.

Focusing on priorities is another essential tactic. Not all emails require a reply, and not every task demands urgent focus. Leaders can reduce stress by recognizing what is genuinely important and prioritizing those tasks initially. An uncomplicated approach, such as categorizing tasks by their urgency and importance, can simplify the decision-making process. This allows leaders to focus their time and energy on what is most essential instead of becoming overwhelmed by the endless demands.

Technology can likewise contribute to the solution. Instruments designed to assist with task management, monitor due dates, and plan concentrated work periods can reduce the burden of maintaining organization. For example, a leader could utilize project management tools to assign tasks, making certain that responsibilities are well distributed and nothing is overlooked. Nonetheless, these tools only prove effective when leaders employ them purposefully. It's not about installing additional apps on your phone. It involves selecting the appropriate tools and employing them to streamline your workflow.

The digital age further highlights the need for leaders to develop multitasking capabilities. With an abundance of information available, leaders frequently feel compelled to manage several tasks simultaneously. They reply to emails while in meetings, shift focus among projects, and answer messages amid crucial tasks. Although this may seem effective, it really lowers productivity and increases mental exhaustion. Studies and my real experience indicate that frequent task-switching reduces efficiency and makes concentrating more challenging. Leaders can address this by reserving distinct periods for focused, uninterrupted work. Even half an hour of concentrated work on one task can enhance productivity and lessen stress.

In addition to techniques and routines, handling stress in the digital era necessitates a change in perspective. Leaders need to understand that being always accessible doesn't enhance their job performance. Actually, it frequently results in exhaustion. Rather than attempting to handle every task, leaders ought to concentrate on their strengths, leading their teams, making strategic choices, and upholding their vision. By taking a step back and having faith in their teams to manage the details, leaders liberate themselves to concentrate on the larger perspective.

Achieving balance in the digital age involves more than just safeguarding oneself. It's about being a role model for your team. When leaders exemplify healthy practices, like unplugging after hours or emphasizing work-life balance, it initiates a ripple effect. Teams feel encouraged to follow suit, reducing stress throughout the organization.

In the end, handling stress in the digital era involves using technology purposefully, rather than allowing it to dominate you. Leaders who assert control over their digital spaces, instead of merely responding to them, can foster a more effective and healthier work environment. The tools are available to assist, yet the decisions you make dictate if they transform into a solution or merely add more stress.

Final Thoughts

Leadership will unavoidably bring its own set of difficulties. Stress, although unavoidable, doesn't need to determine your path. This chapter has demonstrated that stress-free leadership does not equate to perfection or the lack of pressure. It involves learning how to handle stress in ways that help you remain focused, make improved decisions, and uphold balance in your life. The concepts of reimagining success, establishing limits, and adopting resilience equip leaders with the resources to manage stress efficiently and lead with intention.

While contemplating these concepts, think about how stress impacts not just you but also those in your vicinity. Leadership stress isn't limited to a single individual. It extends to your team, your family, and your whole organization. The decisions you make and how you manage stress influence the atmosphere of those around you. Grasping the ripple effects of stress is the next phase in creating a sustainable leadership approach. Let's dive into learning more about stress and how it influences the relationships and interactions in your life.

02

WHAT STRESS DOES TO LEADERS AND THEIR CIRCLES

Stress is not something you face alone. While Chapter 1 focused on how leaders can handle stress, this chapter looks at how it affects others. Stress doesn't stay contained. It spreads, impacting your team, your family, and the entire organization.

When a leader feels stressed, it doesn't escape notice. It influences how they make choices, how they communicate, and the level of interest they contribute to their tasks. Stress can seep into every area of a workplace, diminishing morale and causing tension. At home, it may put a strain on relationships, making it more difficult to bond with those you care about. The impact of stress is extensive, depending on how effectively we manage our stress level.

To grasp the concept of how stress spreads, we must first examine what it truly entails. Stress isn't solely about experiencing being overburdened. Your body and mind respond to difficulties, manifesting in various forms. It could be a racing heartbeat prior to a meeting, sleepless nights filled with anxiety, or irritation during discussions.

These indicators are overlooked until they begin to impact your everyday existence.

This chapter starts by defining stress and how it manifests. Subsequently, we will explore the impact that stress has on you and the people in your vicinity. Stress does not end with the person. It creates a ripple effect, and acknowledging this is the initial step to controlling its influence.

2.1 Understanding Stress

Stress is not merely a temporary sensation of feeling overwhelmed. It's a response, both bodily and psychological, to the pressures imposed on us. For leaders, it frequently serves as a quiet presence, accompanying them during meetings, choices, and engagements. Although it's simple to view stress as merely "a job requirement," neglecting it may result in lasting effects for both leaders and their colleagues.

Take a leader preparing for a major product launch. The stakes are high, and every detail feels critical. Emails begin early in the morning, and messages continue into the night. The pressure to meet deadlines and ensure success is constant. At first, they manage it well. They stay late, skip meals, and power through, thinking they'll make up for it once things settle down. But weeks go by, and the strain doesn't ease. They start to feel drained. The lack of sleep catches up. Minor issues at work irritate them more than they should. Their focus begins to slip, and they feel disconnected at home, unable to engage fully with loved ones. Stress has taken hold.

Stress accumulates over time, frequently without notice. It may begin as something minor, tense shoulders, creating fear, or an overactive mind, and develop into something more difficult to control. Physically, stress can manifest as ongoing headaches, exhaustion, or digestive issues. In terms of mental capacity, it hinders decision-making and diminishes concentration. Emotionally, it causes feelings of irritation, anxiety, or even disconnection. Initially, these signs may appear manageable, but if overlooked, they pile up, forming a cycle that becomes increasingly difficult to escape as time goes on.

What makes stress feel so overpowering? The solution is found in biology. When you experience stress, your body triggers its fight-or-flight reaction. This is how your body gets ready to confront a challenge. Your heart races, your muscles tense, and your mind concentrates on the urgent issue. In brief intervals, this reaction aids in maintaining alertness and excelling under stress. However, when stress is ever-present, your body stays in this elevated state. As time passes, this exhausts you physically, mentally, and emotionally.

For leaders, pressure frequently arises from various sources. External pressures, such as time constraints and elevated expectations, are one aspect of the situation. Internal pressures, such as personal standards and the conviction that they must constantly maintain control, create an additional layer. Leaders frequently feel they need to bear these burdens by themselves, thinking that displaying vulnerability will weaken their power. This way of thinking only intensifies the effects of stress.

Identifying stress is crucial. Numerous leaders overlook the initial indicators, believing they are merely aspects of the role. However, overlooking stress is akin to disregarding the warning signals on your dashboard. The issue doesn't disappear; it escalates. Noticing how stress manifests in your life is the initial step toward managing it. Are you snapping at your team more often than normal? Are you having difficulty with decisions that you would usually consider easy? Do you feel exhausted even after a restful night's sleep? These indicate that stress is having an impact.

Recognizing stress involves recognizing that it is a common experience for everyone. Even the most self-assured and skilled leaders encounter it. Feeling stressed doesn't indicate that you are failing. It signifies that you are human. Understanding this enables you to confront stress without criticism, providing you the opportunity to tackle it positively.

What actions can you take when stress starts to dominate? The initial step is recognizing. Notice the ways stress appears in your life. Pay attention to physical signals, such as body tension or trouble sleeping. Recognize the emotional indicators, such as feeling agitated or easily stressed. Consider the mental indicators, such as difficulty focusing or a sense of being trapped. By identifying these patterns, you can begin to dismantle them.

Stress isn't solely related to how much work you're handling. It concerns the way in which you are executing it. Leaders frequently concentrate on handling their responsibilities without recognizing that they must also manage their energy. Easy adjustments, such as taking pauses, assigning responsibilities, or establishing clear limits, can significantly impact. These changes won't completely remove stress, but they assist you in handling it more healthily.

Leaders are not required to confront stress by themselves. Discussing it with a mentor, coworker, or reliable friend can offer insight and encouragement. Revealing your experiences doesn't weaken you. It demonstrates that you are dedicated to discovering solutions, not only for yourself but also for your team and organization.

Stress is a part of leadership challenges, but it shouldn't determine your path. By grasping its functionality and acknowledging its effects, you can initiate the initial steps to manage it efficiently. Stress is not an obstacle, it's about communication and how we handle it. The more you pay attention to it, the more prepared you'll be to guide with clarity and balance.

2.2 The Effects of Stress

Understanding stress is merely a part of the overall scenario. After you identify its presence in your life, the following step is to observe its impact on you and others nearby. Stress doesn't merely reside within your mind or body. It influences every action you take, from the choices you make to how you engage with others.

Have you ever thought about why stress seems so exhausting? It affects you in every way, mentally, physically, and emotionally. It's not merely about experiencing fatigue or lack of focus. Pressure alters how your brain and body operate. It doesn't end with you. Your stress affects those around you, influencing the morale of your team, the ambiance at home, and even the environment of your workplace.

2.2.1 How it impacts you mentally and physically

Stress isn't confined to your thoughts alone. It circulates throughout your body, impacting mental strength, physical wellness, and emotional health. Stress generates a cycle of excessive pondering and a lack of confidence in oneself. It hinders decision-making, makes even straightforward tasks seem daunting, and diminishes concentration. Physically, stress elevates your body to manage immediate challenges, but when this condition endures, it leads to lasting damage. Leaders, frequently facing ongoing pressure, feel these effects in ways that influence every aspect of their lives.

Studies by the American Psychological Association indicate that stress triggers the hypothalamic-pituitary-adrenal (HPA) axis, leading to the release of hormones such as cortisol and adrenaline. These hormones ready the body to tackle immediate challenges by elevating heart rate, tightening muscles, and enhancing concentration. This reaction is beneficial in brief intervals, but when stress persists, it impacts the brain and body in distinct ways. Research published in The Lancet Psychiatry emphasizes that extended stress can diminish the prefrontal cortex, which is the region linked to decision-making and self-regulation. This illustrates how extended stress can hinder concentration and decision-making, rendering even minor choices seem significant.

In daily life, this psychological pressure manifests as persistent self-doubt, excessive contemplation, and difficulty focusing. Have you ever caught yourself going over a conversation in your head, stressing about what you said or did? That's pressure in the workplace. It generates an illusion of urgency that complicates effective prioritization. This psychological strain not only makes tasks seem more challenging but also leaves you feeling exhausted.

Pressure also impacts the body. The fight-or-flight reaction, activated by stress, is meant to deal with urgent dangers. Your heart beats faster, your breath speeds up, and your muscles tense up to get ready for movement. Nonetheless, when stress is perpetual, this increased condition negatively impacts your physical well-being. Persistent stress has been associated with migraines, gastrointestinal problems, elevated blood pressure, and a compromised immune response. The Mayo Clinic highlights that extended stress may result in exhaustion, sleep issues, and a higher likelihood of severe health problems such as heart disease. It's not only about experiencing fatigue or stress. As time passes, these physical symptoms become increasingly difficult to overlook and may result in long-term health hazards.

Stress also has a profound impact on emotions. Leaders facing stress might end up reacting abruptly with coworkers or showing reduced patience with family and friends. Minor irritations seem more significant than they ought to be, making effective communication more challenging. Stress can create a sense of disconnection from others, contributing an additional layer of emotional burden. These emotional impacts frequently influence physical symptoms in return. Inadequate sleep due to stress results in irritability, which increases tension at home or work, thus continuing the cycle.

Identifying these impacts is the initial move toward controlling stress. The signals your body conveys, such as stress, exhaustion, or trouble focusing, are not signs of weakness. They are signals indicating that something requires attention. Overlooking them doesn't eliminate the stress. Rather, leaders need to recognize these indicators promptly and take steps to stop stress from increasing.

Stress does not signify failure. It's a typical reaction to the challenges of leadership. By grasping its influence on your mental and physical state, you can begin to manage its effects. Minor modifications, such as taking frequent breaks, focusing on important tasks, or just recognizing when you're feeling overwhelmed, can greatly impact your effectiveness. Pressure can be a component of leadership, yet it shouldn't have to characterize it. Acknowledging its influence is the initial step towards establishing healthier routines and a more balanced way of managing your duties.

2.2.2 The way it spreads to your team, family, and organization

Stress impacts not only the individual experiencing it. It quietly affects the areas and connections surrounding them. A leader under stress can unintentionally generate a ripple effect that influences their team, their family, and the larger organization. These impacts extend beyond alterations in mood. They affect trust, communication, and others' capacity to excel.

In a work environment, stress can alter how a team operates. A leader experiencing stress may act sharply, concentrating solely on urgent tasks while overlooking future objectives. This generates doubt for the team. Individuals begin to doubt their choices or hesitate to act, fearing they might make errors. With time, this environment can affect team creativity and drive. Have you ever been in a group where everyone is merely trying to "make it through the day"? This is frequently the outcome of stress flowing downward from higher-ups.

Communication is another domain where stress reveals its impact. Tense leaders may provide vague guidance or overlook crucial information in a bid to expedite the process. This causes confusion and frustration among team members. Poor communication results in wasted effort, missed deadlines, and unnecessary conflicts. The absence of clarity also undermines trust, leading individuals to wonder if their leader possesses a clear strategy or path.

Stress also negatively impacts decision-making. Overwhelmed leaders might rush to conclusions, prioritizing what seems urgent over what genuinely matters. These immediate choices may lead to lasting issues. For instance, a pressured leader may authorize a rapid solution to meet a deadline, only to discover that it creates additional problems later on. This responsive strategy can disrupt the organization, complicating efforts for teams to remain aligned and efficient.

The reach of stress extends beyond the workplace. The consequences at home can be equally harmful. Relatives frequently endure the impact of unmanaged stress. A leader who carries job-related stress at home may find it difficult to be entirely engaged. They may disengage during discussions, become frustrated over trivial matters, or withdraw into quietness. This may cause family and friends to feel overlooked or uncertain about how to assist. As time goes on, these instances accumulate, leading to emotional distance in relationships that previously appeared intimate and nurturing.

Children, especially, are affected by stress within the home. They sense the tension in a parent's tone or physical demeanor, even when no words are used. This may induce anxiety for them, particularly if they are unsure about what is triggering the change. The emotional pressure impacts not only the leader. It generates waves that touch the whole family.

In a workplace setting, the dissemination of stress can alter the culture itself. When leaders work under relentless pressure, they might unintentionally demonstrate that stress and burnout are inherent to the role. This establishes an environment where workers believe they need to be constantly tired and overworked to fulfill demands. While productivity might stay elevated for some time, it does so at a price. Burnout will increase rapidly, employee turnover will rise, and the organization will find it difficult to uphold stability. The organization's long-term well-being deteriorates when stress is normalized.

When stress increases without control, it weakens the fundamental aspects of effective leadership. Confidence level will slowly go down and can result in communication breaks down. Connections, whether in a career or personal life, begin to weaken. These problems may not surface immediately, but as time goes on, their impact becomes difficult to overlook.

Understanding how stress spreads is not solely about safeguarding yourself. It's about fostering healthier surroundings for all those you engage with. Teams flourish when their leader stays calm and consistent. Families become more resilient when stress is confronted rather than suppressed. Organizations excel when their culture prioritizes balance and well-being.

The effects of stress are extensive, yet they don't need to be lasting. Leaders who actively manage their own stress can disrupt the cycle and serve as positive role models for others. This does not imply acting as if stress isn't real. It involves recognizing it and discovering methods to react that lessen its impact on yourself and others nearby.

Final Thoughts

Leadership involves more than just making decisions and achieving results. It's about the way you present yourself each day. Stress is unavoidable, but it doesn't need to determine your journey. It's your body and mind seeking balance.

Stress doesn't stay contained. It affects how you think, how you connect, and the energy you bring to your team and loved ones. Left unchecked, it creates distance, erodes trust, and weakens relationships. But when you take control of stress, the ripple effect changes. You lead with focus. You inspire calm. You build trust and clarity in the spaces around you.

The aim isn't to escape pressure but to handle it in a manner that benefits you and those who depend on you. Leadership without stress does not mean getting rid of challenges. It's about reacting to them purposefully. By prioritizing balance, you foster a space where everyone, including yourself, can flourish.

The next step is turning understanding into action. Let's move forward.

03

MANAGING STRESS WITH A PRACTICAL APPROACH

Stress is part of every leader's journey. It influences your thoughts, your behaviors, and your relationships with others. You've observed how it affects you individually and how it extends to impact your team, family, and organization. However, being aware that stress is present is just part of the struggle. The following step is discovering how to handle it in a manner that suits you.

Stress is individual. Your experience of it and your reactions to it differ from those of others. What burdens one individual may inspire another. Your history, routines, and experiences all influence how stress impacts you and your coping mechanisms. Grasping these distinctions is essential for discovering a practical method that aligns with your lifestyle and leadership approach.

This section examines two significant concepts. Initially, we will examine the reasons that stress management is not a universal solution. You will discover how your individual experiences influence your reactions and why recognizing these distinctions is important. Next, we'll explore typical triggers for leaders, including unfulfilled expectations, demanding deadlines, and the difficulties of managing situations outside your control. By comprehending these triggers, you'll be more prepared to handle them successfully.

Handling stress doesn't imply removing it entirely. This involves discovering methods and resources that assist you in gaining control when things begin to feel too intense. Let's proceed, shall we?

3.1 Why Managing Stress Is Personal

Stress varies from person to person. What difficulties may inspire one individual could encourage another. Have you observed how certain individuals appear to manage stress effortlessly, whereas others find it difficult to remain composed? It's not a matter of being strong or weak. Stress is highly individual. It represents your behaviors, experiences, and the way you have adapted to challenging circumstances.

When stress occurs, how do you respond? Do you dive into resolving issues, wishing to handle everything simultaneously? Or do you feel stuck and uncertain about how to proceed? Perhaps you seek assistance or pause to collect your thoughts. There isn't just one correct method for handling stress, and that's exactly the idea. What is effective for another person may not be effective for you. And that is fine.

Stress is just as individual as the person who feels it. Consider how individuals respond in various ways to identical circumstances. An individual may excel when facing a strict deadline, harnessing the pressure to enhance their concentration. Someone else could feel immobilized, consumed by the relentless passage of time. These distinctions do not concern who is superior or more skilled. They originate from our instincts and the experiences we've encountered.

Have you ever thought about why some situations cause you more stress than others? Perhaps a demanding presentation makes you feel nervous, whereas a quick-moving project can motivate and give you the excitement to perform well. The essential aspect of grasping stress is acknowledging that it is closely linked to your character and previous experiences.

When we measure our responses against those of others, it's simple to perceive that we're lacking. You may observe a coworker remaining composed during a crisis and wonder, "Why can't I be like that?" However, comparisons of this nature overlook the main issue. Each person copes with stress in their own way since individual triggers and reactions are influenced by various factors. Rather than attempting to replicate another person's method, concentrate on what suits you best.

Certain individuals discover comfort in the organization. They must prepare in advance and adhere to schedules to feel stable. Some perform optimally by remaining adaptable and adjusting to challenges as they occur. These are not merely preferences. They are strategies for survival developed over time. If you can identify what suits you, you'll cease pushing yourself into approaches that conflict with your inherent instincts.

Stress is an individual matter because it mirrors your distinct mix of personality, experiences, and ways of coping. Recognizing this relieves the stress of conforming to another person's expectations. You are not required to manage stress in the same manner as another person. You simply have to grasp what is effective for you and embrace it confidently.

3.1.1 Everyone handles stress differently, and that's okay

When we measure our responses against those of others, it's simple to perceive that we're lacking. You may observe a coworker remaining composed during a crisis and wonder, "Why can't I be like that?" However, comparisons of this nature overlook the main issue. Each person copes with stress in their own way since individual triggers and reactions are influenced by various factors. Rather than attempting to replicate another person's method, concentrate on what suits you best.

Certain individuals discover comfort in the organization. They must prepare in advance and adhere to schedules to feel stable. Some perform optimally by remaining adaptable and adjusting to challenges as they occur. These are not merely preferences. They are strategies for survival developed over time. If you can identify what suits you, you'll cease pushing yourself into approaches that conflict with your inherent instincts.

Stress is individual because it mirrors your distinct mix of personality, experiences, and ways of coping. Recognizing this will help mitigate the stress of conforming to another person's expectations. You are not required to manage stress in the same manner as another person. You simply have to grasp what is effective for you and embrace it confidently.

Various individuals employ distinct methods for managing stress. Some depend on the organization. They seek comfort in routines, lists, and well-defined strategies. They require a sense of organization to feel stable. Some flourish with adaptability. They're at ease with adjusting as circumstances evolve and concentrating on the overall perspective instead of the specifics. Both approaches are equally good or bad. They are merely various methods of dealing. The important aspect is recognizing what feels suitable for you.

Stress impacts you differently on each occasion. It varies based on the circumstances. You could feel motivated by the demands of a rapidly moving project yet entirely exhausted by a challenging discussion with a coworker. You may manage work-related stress effectively but find it difficult to cope with personal issues, or vice versa. These distinctions are not defects. They contribute to your uniqueness.

When you attempt to impose another person's approach to managing stress on yourself, it frequently leads to negative outcomes. It may result in feelings of frustration or potentially heightened overwhelm. Rather than concentrating on what benefits others, invest time in discovering what benefits you. Be mindful of your responses in various situations. Do you take time to think things through before acting, or do you like to confront challenges directly? Do you feel a greater sense of control when adhering to a plan, or do you prefer the comfort of adapting along the way? These patterns contain the solutions to effectively managing your stress.

How you manage stress showcases your character, your past experiences, and the techniques you've cultivated over the years. It's individual, and that's not merely acceptable, it's something to welcome. You don't have to conform to another person's vision of how stress management ought to appear. All you need is to comprehend your own method and ensure it functions effectively for you.

Stress is an unavoidable aspect of life, yet it doesn't need to dominate you. By releasing comparisons and concentrating on what maintains your balance, you can develop a healthier and more efficient response method. When stress becomes too much, remind yourself that it's not about doing it the "correct" way. It's about executing it in your style.

3.1.2 How your experiences shape your response

Stress doesn't just happen. The way you react to it is shaped by the life you've lived, the lessons you've learned, and the challenges you've overcome. Every experience leaves a mark, creating patterns that influence how you deal with pressure today. These patterns aren't random. They're deeply connected to your personal history, and understanding them can change the way you handle stress.

Think about your early years. Was stress something your family talked about openly? Or was it brushed aside, something to be ignored? If you grew up in an environment where people calmly addressed problems, you might feel more comfortable tackling stress head-on. But if you were surrounded by conflict or silence, you might find yourself avoiding difficult situations or feeling uneasy when pressure builds. Neither response is better or worse. They're reflections of what you learned during those formative years.

Reflect on how these initial teachings manifest in your life today. Do you notice that you respond to stress in the same manner as a parent or mentor used to? Perhaps you learned to suppress your feelings because that was your upbringing. Or maybe you cultivated a tendency to address issues right away due to recognizing the importance of prompt responses. These replies are not coincidental. They are routines you have developed gradually.

Your work experiences contribute to this as well. Have you been in situations that excel under intense pressure, where stress was considered typical? Or have you held positions that promoted balance and allowed you the freedom to handle your workload? If you've spent years in a high-pressure role, you may have created tactics to manage ongoing expectations. However, you might have also developed habits that make it more difficult to handle stress, such as taking on too many commitments or pushing yourself excessively. Your strengths and challenges arise from the environments you have been a part of.

Think about a situation that felt particularly stressful. What triggered it? Was it a last-minute deadline, a difficult conversation, or something out of your control? Now, think about how you responded. Did you focus on fixing the problem immediately? Did you step back to gather your thoughts? Or did you feel stuck, unsure of where to begin? These patterns matter. They reveal the strategies you've built over time and the areas where you might need more support.

Your narrative influences your reaction to stress. That's what gives it a personal touch. Nobody else has experienced your life or confronted your difficulties. This is the reason that measuring yourself against others is unhelpful. Concentrate on what benefits you. You might require structure to feel centered, or perhaps flexibility is essential for your tranquility. There isn't just one formula. The correct method is the one that aligns with your individual experiences and requirements.

Comprehending how your history impacts your current situation does not involve placing blame. It's about obtaining understanding. Upon recognizing the link between your experiences and your responses, you can begin to implement deliberate modifications. Rather than responding instinctively, you can take a moment to pause, think, and select a reaction that corresponds with your objectives.

Stress is a normal part of life, yet it should not dominate you. By understanding how your narrative influences your reaction, you can control how you manage stress. This is not about altering your identity. It involves gaining a deeper insight into yourself and utilizing that insight to lead with assurance and precision.

3.2 What Triggers Stress for Leaders

Stress doesn't occur without a cause. It arises from particular circumstances or difficulties that extend your limits beyond what seems controllable. For leaders, these triggers frequently arise from the demands of achieving goals, directing teams, and maintaining accountability.

Identifying what triggers your stress is a crucial initial step. Once you comprehend the triggers, you can start tackling the root issues rather than merely responding to the symptoms.

What circumstances make you feel the most worried? Is it when expectations fail to align, when communication falters, or when a challenge occurs that is completely beyond your influence? These triggers frequently emphasize what is most important to you as a leader. They indicate where you are working to achieve objectives and where the burden of responsibility feels the greatest.

Let's examine several typical stressors that leaders encounter. Unfulfilled expectations and strict timelines, misunderstandings and unforeseen obstacles, along with issues that seem largely out of your control, are several of the main problems that arise repeatedly. By comprehending the impact of these stressors on you, you can equip yourself to manage them with improved clarity and confidence.

3.2.1 Unmet expectations and tight deadlines

There are few experiences as stressful as recognizing that you're not meeting expectations, whether those expectations are from others or from yourself. As a leader, the pressure always seems intense. You may establish challenging objectives for your team or commit to a delivery schedule that allows no space for setbacks. However, when events don't unfold as expected, the stress can seem intense.

Consider an occasion when a deadline approached more rapidly than you anticipated. Perhaps a vital piece of information was postponed, or an unexpected hurdle hindered advancement. Did you sense the pressure of attempting to restore everything to order? Deadlines may serve as a continual reminder of what is at risk, while unfulfilled expectations intensify that pressure. It's not solely about achieving a target; it's about preserving trust and credibility with those who rely on you.

The pressure of unfulfilled expectations extends beyond timelines. It frequently connects to a greater feeling of responsibility. You may feel as though you are disappointing your team or not achieving the expectations you have established for yourself. These emotions can escalate, causing you to wonder if you could have accomplished more or organized things more effectively.

To handle this stress, it's essential to keep in mind that no plan is flawless. Timelines and anticipations are not always under your influence. By concentrating on what you can affect, be it enhancing communication or dividing tasks into smaller, more achievable steps, you can lighten or relieve the stress and regain a feeling of control.

3.2.2 Miscommunication and Unexpected Challenges

Misunderstanding is one of the main causes of stress for leaders. One small miscommunication can derail an entire project. Have you ever been in a scenario where you believed everyone was on the same page, only to realize that important aspects were misinterpreted? The confusion and frustration that arise can rapidly result in stress.

Unforeseen obstacles introduce an additional level of complexity. These are the times when an unforeseen event disrupts your plan completely. It could be an unexpected shift in priorities, an essential team member becoming unavailable, or an outside factor hindering progress. These obstacles require you to adapt quickly, which can be daunting when both time and resources are constrained.

Both miscommunication and unforeseen difficulties challenge your capacity to adjust. They need fast reasoning and clear expression. However, in the midst of the situation, it's simple to sense that everything is slipping away from you. You may be concerned about maintaining the team's focus or how to communicate the delays to stakeholders.

The secret to handling this stress is maintaining focus on solutions. Rather than focusing on what went wrong or things happened not as plan, consider what actions can be taken to progress. Effective communication is crucial. By clarifying roles, resetting expectations, or just recognizing the challenge, taking proactive steps can assist you and your team in regaining momentum.

3.2.3 Problems beyond your control

One of the most aggravating sources of stress is handling issues that are completely beyond your control. These are the circumstances where no level of planning or effort could have avoided the problem. It could be a change in market dynamics that alters priorities, a technology issue, or an unforeseen occurrence beyond the organization. The absence of control can make you feel helpless, and this sensation significantly contributes to stress.

When encountering issues like these, it's usual to feel trapped. You may revisit the scenario in your thoughts, contemplating if there was anything you overlooked or ought to have approached differently. However, the truth is that not all things are under your control. The pressure arises from the belief that you ought to solve everything, even when it isn't feasible.

Leaders frequently assume a significant amount of responsibility for themselves. You may believe that you have to address every issue to demonstrate your skills or to help the team progress. However, this strategy can have negative consequences. Taking on too much can increase stress levels and complicate the path to finding solutions.

The most effective method to handle this kind of stress is to concentrate on what you can influence. Recognize the aspects where you can contribute, and release the others. It's not about surrendering, it's about understanding that your efforts are better directed towards actions that foster advancement. By changing your focus, you'll discover it's simpler to overcome frustration and pursue solutions.

Final Thoughts

Stress is part of leadership, but it doesn't have to overwhelm you. This chapter has explored how personal experiences and responses shape your stress management and how common triggers like unmet expectations, miscommunication, and uncontrollable situations add pressure. The key takeaway is that managing stress begins with understanding yourself, how you react, what affects you most, and which strategies help you regain control.

When you take the time to recognize your unique stress patterns and the triggers that intensify them, you open the door to practical solutions. Whether it's adjusting your approach to deadlines, improving communication with your team, or learning to focus only on what you can control, the steps you take will bring you closer to leading with confidence and balance.

This foundation naturally leads to the next step, strengthening your ability to handle stress. Understanding your triggers is only the beginning. Chapter 4 will take a deeper look at how you can build resilience, plan proactively to reduce pressure and change the way you approach challenges. It's not just about managing stress but also about turning it into an opportunity for growth and leadership clarity. Let's continue this journey.

04

STRENGTHENING YOUR ABILITY TO HANDLE STRESS

Leadership involves stress, but your response to it can make a significant difference. It's not solely about identifying moments when you feel overwhelmed. It involves making preparations, reacting with composure, and remaining stable under increasing pressure. This section will demonstrate how to accomplish that. We will start by concentrating on self-awareness. What causes your stress? What causes some circumstances to impact you more than others? Understanding these answers allows you to generate responses that suit your preferences and requirements.

Next, we will discuss the preparation. Have you ever encountered a stressful scenario and wondered, "This might have been simpler if I had organized better"? Some planning can lessen unwanted stress and make you feel more in charge when things become hectic. We will examine how altering your viewpoint can create an impact. Do you view setbacks as failures, or do you consider them as chances to learn?

Changing your perspective on challenges can assist you in progressing, even when events don't unfold as expected.

Finally, we will address emotional reactions. Pressure frequently influences the way you interact with others. Have you ever expressed something out of frustration and later wished you hadn't? Developing the ability to respond calmly can enhance your relationships and enable you to manage stressful situations more efficiently.

4.1 Knowing Yourself

Do you sometimes wonder why some situations make you feel overwhelmed while others do not? Stress impacts individuals differently, which contributes to its personal nature. The triggers of your stress are influenced by your experiences, values, and also your everyday routines. Recognizing these triggers is the initial step toward managing them successfully.

Pressure frequently creeps up on you. At one point, everything seems under control, and the next, you find it hard to maintain your concentration. What occurred? Was it an unforeseen email containing unfortunate news? Perhaps it was a gathering that didn't unfold as expected. These instances may seem intense, yet they contain important hints. Identifying the triggers of your stress is akin to discovering the final piece of a jigsaw. It aids in recognizing the source of the pressure and the actions you can take in response.

Have you ever observed how certain situations appear to upset you more than others? Perhaps a missed deadline seems like the end of the world, while a postponed project doesn't bother you. Or maybe a remark from a coworker lingers in your mind for days, even if it was not intended to be harmful. These variations are not coincidental. They are linked to how your brain handles specific situations and how your previous experiences shape your responses.

Consider a moment when a minor concern escalated into a significantly larger issue. Did it resonate with you because it brought to mind a comparable challenge you've encountered previously? Stress does not occur in a vacuum. It links to your aspirations, your objectives, and also your anxieties. Perhaps you set high standards for yourself, making unmet expectations feel like a personal shortcoming. Or maybe you've faced comparable challenges before, and they evoke feelings of annoyance or concern. Understanding why something influences you enables a response that seems deliberate rather than simply reactive.

Self-awareness doesn't arrive suddenly. It involves being aware of your feelings and observing trends over a period. When stress strikes again, take a moment to pause. How do you feel? Is it irritation, anxiety, or a feeling of being overpowered? After identifying the emotion, reflect on why it feels so powerful. What is it about this scenario that provokes such an intense reaction? You might be surprised by the answers.

Knowing yourself goes beyond merely identifying stress. It's about understanding how to apply that knowledge to improve decision-making. When you understand your triggers, you can begin to foresee difficult situations and handle them in a different way. Rather than being taken by surprise, you can equip yourself mentally and emotionally.

You may decide to establish clearer limits, request assistance, or alter your perspective on the challenge ahead.

4.1.1 Recognizing What Triggers Your Stress and Why

What triggers your stress? Is it tight deadlines, unexpected criticism, or the fear of letting others down? Take a moment to think about the situations that make your heart race or leave you feeling drained. These triggers are unique to you, shaped by your experiences and how you interpret the world around you.

Imagine a leadership meeting where someone questions your decision. For one person, this might feel like a chance to clarify their thinking and move on. For another, it could feel like an attack, sparking doubt and worry about their competence. Neither reaction is better or worse. They are personal, reflecting how you approach challenges and the expectations you carry.

Recognizing your triggers isn't just about naming what stresses you. It's about digging into the reasons behind those feelings. Why do deadlines leave you feeling in fear? Is it because you've always equated meeting deadlines with success? Why does conflict in the workplace unsettle you? Maybe it's because you value harmony and fear confrontation might damage relationships. These are not just surface-level reactions. They are tied to deeper beliefs and experiences.

Think back to a recent moment when stress caught you off guard. What exactly happened? Was it a situation where things felt out of control? Did it bring up emotions like frustration, fear, or even embarrassment? Now, go deeper. What was it about that situation that hit so hard? Was it tied to your desire to meet high standards, or was it the uncertainty of not knowing how to handle the situation? These reflections are essential. They help you understand not just the "what" but the "why."

Once you identify your triggers, you can begin to control them in a manner that feels intentional. Rather than responding quickly without thinking, take a moment to reflect. For instance, if you're aware that strict deadlines stress you out, you could opt to divide the project into smaller tasks to foster a feeling of advancement. If you notice that conflict disturbs you, you may practice a discussion beforehand to feel better equipped.

Understanding your triggers enables you to foresee difficult situations. If you recognize that public speaking increases your stress, you can develop habits to feel more assured, such as starting with smaller groups for practice. If you recognize that sudden changes disrupt your stability, you can establish a routine that assists you in quickly regaining your focus.

Recognizing your triggers doesn't imply completely steering clear of them. Challenging situations will continue to occur. The aim is to acknowledge these instances for what they represent, chances to respond thoughtfully instead of reacting impulsively. When you tackle stress with this perspective, you're not merely handling it. You're managing its impact on you and determining your next steps.

4.2 Planning Ahead

Stress frequently feels overpowering as it can take you by surprise. Have you ever encountered a deadline or circumstance and wished, "If only I had additional time to get ready"? That feeling of not being ready can transform even minor obstacles into larger ones. While planning in advance won't eliminate stress completely, it can reduce a significant amount of avoidable pressure. By making deliberate choices, you can prevent the panic of last-minute rushes and establish a sense of command over your time and energy.

Planning does not equate to striving for perfection. It's about equipping yourself with the resources to manage the unforeseen. Life and leadership seldom adhere to a plan, yet some preparation can significantly impact outcomes. It's similar to embarking on a journey with a guide rather than meandering without direction. While the map may not foresee every hurdle, it will help steer you in the right direction when situations deviate from your expectations.

Have you ever predicted that a task would take less time than it actually does? You might have believed you could complete something in an hour, only to discover midway that it would take twice as long. Such a miscalculation occurs frequently; however, it's also among the simplest causes of stress to address. By incorporating additional time into your timetable, you establish a cushion that shields you from experiencing pressure. If everything proceeds without a hitch, you gain extra time. If they fail to do so, you remain ahead of the game.

Thinking in advance involves more than merely time. It concerns clarity. Have you ever begun a project only to find out halfway through that the expectations were unclear? Poor communication may result in wasted effort and increased stress. Spending a little time at the start to define priorities, deadlines, and responsibilities can prevent hours of frustration further down the line. A straightforward question such as, "How does success appear for this task?" can give you the clarity required to proceed with assurance.

Your physical and mental surroundings also significantly influence your preparation. Is your work environment aiding your concentration, or is it contributing to your distractions? A messy desk, incessant alerts, or a packed inbox can deplete your energy even before you start. Spending time to arrange your area and establish limits for your workday enables you to foster an atmosphere that enhances your productivity rather than obstructing it.

Have you ever faced an extensive to-do list and felt like you were going in circles, attempting to accomplish everything simultaneously? This is where the importance of prioritization arises. Begin by listing all the tasks you need to complete, and then prioritize them based on their significance. Prioritize the most important one initially. Finishing it not only provides a feeling of advancement but also lessens the mental clutter of attempting to hold everything in your mind simultaneously.

Even minor tasks, such as getting ready the evening prior to an important meeting or creating a checklist for a project, can have an impact. These actions may appear trivial, but they accumulate. They ease the cognitive burden of recalling every detail and provide you with a straightforward plan to stick to as the pressure increases.

Rest periods are another aspect of planning that frequently go unnoticed. How frequently have you worked during lunch or missed a break to push through your duties? Taking breaks isn't wasting time, it's about conserving energy. A brief five-minute stroll, a cup of water, or just a moment of silence can help rejuvenate your concentration and maintain your productivity all day.

Anticipating future events doesn't guarantee that your timetable will consistently proceed without issues. Obstacles will continue to appear. However, with proper preparation, you will be more prepared to manage them without becoming overloaded. A bit of planning can help you avoid a great deal of stress. It's not about possessing an ideal strategy. It's about establishing the environment necessary for clear thinking and responding assertively when challenges arise.

4.2.1 Effective Ways to Avoid Unnecessary Pressure

Begin by examining your everyday tasks. Are there responsibilities you can streamline or assign to someone else? At times, stress arises from attempting to handle too many things simultaneously. Dividing bigger tasks into smaller, more achievable steps can have a significant impact. For instance, rather than trying to finish an entire project in a single session, concentrate on completing one section at a time. This fosters a feeling of advancement and allows the workload to seem less daunting.

Another method to manage pressure is by establishing achievable expectations. Are you allowing yourself sufficient time to finish tasks, or are you filling your agenda so tightly that there's no space for adaptability? Think about incorporating additional time for unforeseen setbacks. If you believe a task will require an hour, prepare for an hour and a half. That additional buffer can spare you from unwarranted stress if things don't unfold as expected.

Communication significantly contributes to effective planning for the future. Have you ever consented to undertake a task without completely grasping what is needed? Misinterpretations like these can result in lost time and increased stress. Pause briefly to outline deadlines, expectations, and priorities prior to beginning. Inquire if anything is unclear. Direct communication at the beginning can avoid issues afterward.

Your surroundings are important as well. Is your workspace arranged to aid your concentration, or is it cluttered with distractions? A disorganized desk or frequent distractions can turn straightforward tasks into daunting challenges. Spend a few minutes daily to tidy up your area. Disable unneeded notifications and establish limits with others regarding when you require peace for focus. These minor tweaks can foster a more comfortable atmosphere, facilitating focus on goals.

Have you ever experienced managing several responsibilities simultaneously, only to realize that you're not advancing in any of them? At that moment, prioritization is essential. List your daily tasks and prioritize them by significance. Begin with the highest priority task and proceed to the next one. Concentrating on a single task at a time enables you to feel more in command and lessens the mental confusion of attempting to tackle everything simultaneously.

Finally, don't forget to plan some relaxation time. When you're occupied, it's easy to overlook breaks, but they are essential for sustaining productivity. Spending five minutes to stretch or step away from your screen can rejuvenate your energy and improve your focus. Adding breaks to your routine doesn't imply you're squandering time; it signifies you're gaining the concentration needed to boost your efficiency.

Thinking ahead doesn't ensure you'll evade all obstacles, but it aids in managing them more smoothly. By preparing carefully, you create a pathway to success, regardless of what challenges the day presents.

4.3 Changing How You See Challenges

Obstacles are a natural aspect of life and leadership. They manifest in ways that challenge your patience, your ability to solve issues, and your capacity to remain calm. They might encourage you to reconsider your plans or handle circumstances in a way that differs from what you expected. But what if challenges were more than mere problems to resolve? What if these were chances to evolve? The manner in which you present these circumstances can significantly impact the outcome. Altering your perspective on setbacks can transform both your reaction and the result.

When situations don't unfold as intended, annoyance can dominate. Have you ever encountered a circumstance that seemed like a total disaster at the time, only to later understand that it provided an opportunity you hadn't thought of? These instances hold great significance as they impart valuable lessons to us regarding our circumstances, our decisions, and even our own identities. Development doesn't occur when everything goes perfectly. It arises from overcoming challenges and uncovering new strengths during the journey.

Reflect on your personal experiences. When was the most recent occasion something didn't turn out as you expected? Did you feel trapped? Perhaps you dedicated hours to resolving the problem or felt discouraged for days afterward. Consider what resulted from that moment. Did it assist you in recognizing a region where you might enhance? Did it encourage you to attempt another method that was more effective? These thoughts can alter your approach to obstacles in the future.

Obstacles are not barriers. They are assessments of creativity, patience, and persistence. Seeing them as stepping stones instead of obstacles doesn't imply ignoring their difficulty. It signifies acknowledging their capacity to educate and bring change.

4.3.1 Turning setbacks into opportunities to grow

Have you ever experienced a strategy collapsing despite your greatest attempts? Perhaps a project failed to meet its goals, or a discussion didn't turn out as you anticipated. In those moments, it's simple to feel overwhelmed. But what if, rather than concentrating on the failure, you sought to discover what the experience might impart?

Every obstacle carries a lesson if you're open to seeking it. Did the unachieved goal indicate areas where your process might enhance? Did the challenging discussion uncover a region where communication might be more distinct? Although these moments may be uncomfortable, they can foster growth if you take the time to contemplate them.

Consider a person who motivates you. It's likely that they've encountered obstacles that put them to the test. Successful leaders frequently identify their hardest experiences as the ones that had the greatest impact on their development. It's not about acting like challenges don't affect us. It's about inquiring within, "What can I derive from this?" That change in mindset transforms frustration into concentration.

The next time you face a setback, give this a try. Take a moment to reflect and pose three basic questions to yourself. What occurred? What actions can I take differently next time? What lesson did this impart regarding myself or the circumstances? Jotting down your responses can aid in clarifying the situation and transforming it into something beneficial.

Setbacks are not obstacles. They serve as reminders that there's always an opportunity to learn and enhance. When you view them in this manner, they diminish their ability to restrain you.

4.3.2 Staying flexible when things don't go as planned

Plans are excellent, yet life doesn't always adhere to them. Have you ever crafted an ideal plan or approach, only to see it disrupted by an unforeseen turn? It occurs to all. The crucial aspect is understanding how to adjust while remaining focused on your objectives.

Flexibility doesn't mean abandoning structure. It's about being open to adapting when circumstances shift. Consider you're managing a team, and an essential resource is no longer accessible. Do you freak out, or do you seek out options? Remaining composed and thinking innovatively can transform what seems like a setback into a chance to discover a better way ahead.

A method to maintain flexibility is by concentrating on what you have the ability to manage. When unforeseen difficulties occur, it's simple to feel overwhelmed by all that is not going right. However, focusing on the steps you can take allows you to continue progressing. Is it possible for you to change the order of task priorities? Could you request assistance? Minor changes and improvements can lead to significant changes.

Being flexible also means releasing the pursuit of perfection. Have you ever attempted to adhere to a plan so strictly that it created more stress than it alleviated? At times, the most effective solutions arise when you are flexible and consider an alternative method. It's not about giving up on your aspirations, it's about discovering different methods to achieve them.

When situations don't unfold as expected, consider asking yourself, "What's the best next action I can take?" Concentrating on the specific steps you can undertake anchors you and allows you to progress intentionally. Flexibility doesn't imply you must embrace every change that occurs. It signifies being receptive to the opportunities that change may offer.

4.4 Improving Emotional Responses

Stress affects not only your thoughts but also your choices. It alters your interactions with other people. Have you ever lashed out at someone on a difficult day and felt guilty later? Or perhaps you've steered clear of a discussion because you felt too burdened to manage it. Such instances can harm relationships and generate unwarranted tension, even if that is not your intention. Managing emotions with care involves more than just remaining composed; it requires recognizing how your words and actions impact those around you.

How you feel emotionally influences how others see you. Reflect on a moment when a leader you admired managed a challenging situation with poise. Did it instill assurance? Now think about the reverse, a leader who allows their frustration to erupt. How did that affect your emotions? Whether at work or at home, how you handle stress significantly affects those around you. Through practice, you can master the ability to manage your emotions and react in ways that foster trust, minimize conflict, and maintain open communication.

Why does stress make it more difficult to manage emotional responses? This is due to stress elevating your body and mind, facilitating impulsive reactions. A minor disagreement can seem like a personal assault. A small annoyance can seem daunting and can make us feel worried and tensed. However, these responses aren't fixed. By taking a pause and connecting with your feelings, you can change your reactions in the present.

4.4.1 Staying Calm and Understanding Others Better

Have you ever found yourself in an intense debate and sensed your feelings escalating? Perhaps you desired to protect yourself or react right away. In these instances, the toughest action to take is to stop, but it's also the most impactful. A moment of silence gives you the chance to reflect, inhale deeply, and consider your response before acting. Just a few seconds can determine the contrast between a reflective reply and a rash reaction.

Remaining composed begins with recognizing your feelings. What emotions do you experience when faced with pressure? Does your tone increase in volume? Are you interrupting more often? Identifying these symptoms is the initial move to managing them effectively. When you recognize what's taking place, you can make deliberate decisions rather than allowing your feelings to dictate the dialogue.

Hearing also significantly contributes to handling emotions. Have you ever been so intent on supporting your argument that you overlooked what the other individual was expressing? Listening involves more than simply hearing words. It's about comprehending the emotions that underlie them. Make an effort to pay attention to the tone and body language of the other individual. Are they feeling annoyed? Confused and worried? These signals assist you in reacting with understanding rather than responding defensively.

Comprehending others doesn't imply that you need to concur with them. This signifies recognizing their viewpoint and demonstrating your readiness to participate. For instance, rather than stating, "You're incorrect," consider saying, "I understand your perspective, but allow me to share my opinion." This straightforward change can transform a disagreement into a constructive dialogue.

When feelings run deep, it can be simple to allow stress to dominate. However, by remaining composed, paying close attention, and replying considerately, you establish an environment where genuine communication can take place. These minor adjustments not only alleviate stress but also enhance your connections with others.

Final Thoughts

Stress is an aspect of leadership that cannot be avoided, but the way you manage it defines your path. This chapter emphasized effective methods to recognize your triggers, prepare in advance, change your viewpoint, and enhance your emotional reactions. Every one of these tools is intended to assist you in tackling challenges with composure and perspective, even when situations seem daunting.

Consider what you have discovered up until now. Identifying your stress triggers isn't about evading them, it's about mastering how you react. Thinking ahead provides you with guidance and helps to prevent unnecessary stress. Altering your perspective on setbacks transforms challenges into chances, aiding your development as a leader. Enhancing your emotional reactions bolsters the way you relate to others, both in professional settings and in your personal life.

Leadership without stress doesn't equate to a life without stress. It involves forming habits and tactics that assist you in handling stress in ways that improve your leadership. Each action you make expands upon the last, linking what you've discovered in this chapter to the resources and knowledge we've examined throughout the book.

As we progress, keep this in mind, leadership is a journey. Each challenge presents a chance to enhance your thinking, planning, and reactions. The abilities you develop today will benefit you not only in stressful situations but throughout your entire leadership journey. Let's keep examining ways to lead with greater confidence and reduced stress.

05

TOOLS AND TECHNIQUES TO REDUCE AND MANAGE STRESS

Leadership frequently requires a great deal, and as we've observed, handling stress involves achieving a balance and equipping yourself with effective strategies. At this point, you have investigated how stress affects not only yourself but also your surroundings. You have understood the significance of self-awareness, strategizing, and changing viewpoints when difficulties occur. This chapter expands on those insights and aims to provide you with practical, effective tools to reduce the weight of stress.

Imagine having a set of tools prepared for times when tension begins to increase. What if you could calm your mind with easy methods? What if you had structures to manage your time and a network of support to rely on during challenging times? These concepts are not theoretical. They are genuine, proven methods that anyone can utilize.

We'll begin with techniques you can employ to ground yourself, such as mindfulness practices and physical activities that refresh your energy. Next, we will examine ways to utilize your time more effectively. Are you focusing on what really counts? Are you assigning tasks to prevent feeling overburdened? Finally, we'll examine the benefits of possessing a support system. Leadership doesn't imply shouldering every responsibility by oneself. At times, distributing the burden creates a significant impact.

This section focuses on simplicity. It concerns minor adjustments that lead to enduring outcomes. As you explore these tools and techniques, consider how they might integrate into your everyday routine. The aim is not perfection. It's discovering what suits you best. Let's begin.

5.1 Practical Methods

Stress can feel overwhelming, but it doesn't have to take over. At times, the simplest solutions are the most effective ones. When life seems chaotic, how do you recharge? What actions do you pursue to discover a moment of peace or restore concentration? This part focuses on effective techniques that assist you in soothing your mind and revitalizing your energy.

Leadership challenges can stretch you to your extremes, making you question, "How do I start addressing this?" This is where utilizing straightforward, efficient tools can make a significant difference. Picture having the ability to pause, breathe, and reboot without requiring hours or expert training. Methods such as mindful breathing and participating in physical activities aren't merely practices, they're anchors that rescue you from turmoil and provide you with clarity. Let's look into these techniques together and discover how they can integrate into your daily life.

5.1.1 Easy Ways to Calm Your Mind

Have you ever found yourself difficult or feel like not breathing during a stressful situation? Or experienced your thoughts racing, unable to calm down? Stress frequently leads to a physical reaction before you become aware of it mentally. That's where exercises for breathing are useful. An act as straightforward as engaging in a few deep breaths can transition your body from stress mode to a more relaxed state.

"Take a deep breath." How often have you heard that? However, have you ever genuinely attempted it? Let's get it done now. Breathe in deeply through your nose for a count of four, retain your breath for another four seconds, then breathe out gently through your mouth for a count of six. What is that like? Did your shoulders ease up just a bit? This straightforward method, known as controlled breathing, communicates to your nervous system that it's safe to relax. It requires little time, yet the effect is instant.

A healthy mind and a balanced life offer an effective method to relieve yourself from stressful environments. Have you ever experienced being so immersed in your thoughts that you hardly recognized what was taking place around you? Mindfulness aids in returning your focus to the current moment. Picture yourself sitting still for a single minute, concentrating on the feeling of your feet connecting with the ground or the sound of your breath. "It seems overly simplistic to be effective," you may remark, but that's what makes it beautiful. You're not attempting to repair anything. You're simply allowing your mind a pause from continuously tackling issues.

If you're uncertain about how to begin with mindfulness, think about trying a guided exercise. Numerous applications provide brief sessions, ideal for hectic leaders. Alternatively, you can just set a timer for several minutes, shut your eyes, and concentrate on your breath. The aim isn't to halt your thoughts but to recognize them and allow them to flow by without criticism. Through practice, this can turn into a daily routine that keeps you centered regardless of what challenges the day presents.

These methods don't require perfection. You don't need to perfect them or spend hours practicing. The crucial aspect is to apply them regularly, particularly as stress begins to rise. They provide you with the opportunity to stop, gather your thoughts, and proceed with greater clarity.

5.1.2 Physical Activities and Hobbies That Help You Recharge and Divert Yourself from Stressful Tasks

Stress often traps us in a loop of overthinking, making even simple problems feel overwhelming. What is the most effective method to disrupt that pattern? Take a step back, shift your body, or engage in something you love. Physical activities and hobbies provide more than mere distraction, they rejuvenate your mind and body, making you more equipped to face challenges.

Recall the last occasion you enjoyed your hobbies or engaged in a sport you're passionate about. Didn't you sense a bit more lightness afterward? Physical activities are effective as they redirect your attention from mental stress to bodily movement. Whether it's working out at the gym, jogging outside, or just stretching at home, these actions release natural feel-good chemicals like endorphins in your brain that elevate your mood and relieve stress. A brief session of exercise can make you feel revitalized and more empowered.

However, you aren't required to stick to conventional exercise routines. A few of the most efficient stress-relievers are activities that seem enjoyable. Moving around your home to your beloved playlist, engaging in a game of catch with your children, or simply taking your dog for a stroll in the neighborhood can do wonders. The crucial aspect is movement, anything that shifts your focus from your mind to your body.

Hobbies also play a significant role in reducing and managing stress. Have you ever observed how time appears to pass quickly when you're engaged in something enjoyable? This is due to the fact that hobbies offer a mental escape, enabling you to concentrate on something entirely distinct from your regular duties. Engaging in activities like sports, painting, gardening, playing an instrument, or trying out a new recipe allows you to rejuvenate while partaking in something that feels significant.

What pastimes do you engage in when you seek a break? If you're uncertain, consider the activities that cause you to forget about time. It could be enjoying a great novel, playing golf, playing football, gardening, traveling, or creating something manually. These actions not only distract you from stress, but they also reconnect you with what you love, reintroducing joyful moments into your daily life.

Integrating physical activity with hobbies can yield even greater benefits. Try joining a hiking or cycling club or going fishing with a group of anglers. These actions involve both your body and mind, developing a sense of stability that aids in managing stress more efficiently.

A great aspect of hobbies and physical activities is that they can require very little time. Sometimes, just 10 to 15 minutes of engaging in something you enjoy or being physically active can change your outlook. The secret is to establish a routine, consistently setting aside moments for yourself, regardless of how hectic your day becomes.

Physical activities and hobbies serve as more than mere diversions. They serve as resources to assist you in refreshing and revitalizing, providing you with the vigor and insight needed to face whatever lies ahead.

5.2 Organizing Your Time

Pressure increases when time appears to be an enemy. Do you frequently ponder where your day has gone and why you still feel like you're catching up? Effective time management isn't focused on fitting more activities into your timetable. It's about making intentional decisions that correspond with your objectives. The greater control you possess over your day, the less stress you will experience.

Consider your usual workday. How frequently do you begin with a strategy only to discover it disrupted by distractions or unforeseen problems? Does it make you rush to stay on track? Managing your time can assist in changing that sensation. It provides insight into what requires your focus and aids in eliminating distractions.

We will look at two effective methods. The initial emphasis is on establishing priorities and achievable objectives. The second examines the effectiveness of delegation and how relinquishing certain duties can reduce your burden without sacrificing quality.

5.2.1 Prioritizing Tasks and Setting Realistic Goals

Do you sometimes feel that your to-do list goes on forever? It's simple to get caught in the habit of agreeing to everything only to realize you're swamped. Have you attempted to handle several tasks simultaneously and found that you achieved less?

Begin with this inquiry, "What requires my urgent focus today?" By recognizing the most urgent tasks, you can focus on what really counts. Jotting down your priorities and dividing big tasks into smaller, more manageable steps can lead to significant improvements. For instance, rather than striving to "finish the project," establish a target to "complete the initial draft" or "analyze essential data." Taking smaller steps feels attainable and creates momentum.

It's crucial to establish achievable objectives. Have you ever established an unrealistic deadline for yourself and then felt disheartened when you failed to meet it? Unachievable objectives create extra pressure. Rather, allow yourself space to thrive. Finishing three significant tasks effectively is much more valuable than hurrying through ten and leaving them incomplete.

Thinking in advance is beneficial, too. Dedicate a few minutes every morning to go over your agenda. Are there tasks that can be postponed until later? Are you taking on too many responsibilities? Using this time for planning isn't a waste, it's a commitment to your tranquility.

Don't forget to leave room for the unexpected. Life doesn't follow a perfect script, and building in buffers can save you from last-minute panic. Have you ever felt relief when you had extra time to handle an unforeseen issue? That's the power of planning with flexibility in mind.

5.2.2 Delegating Work So You're Not Doing Everything Alone

What makes it difficult for so many leaders to seek assistance? Is it anxiety that the work might not fulfill their expectations? Or maybe it's the notion that managing everything on your own demonstrates your competence. However, the reality is that attempting to manage everything by oneself frequently results in exhaustion.

Delegation isn't merely about transferring tasks to reduce your workload. It's about distributing responsibilities in a manner that is advantageous for both you and your team. Consider the activities that take up your time yet don't inherently demand your specialized knowledge. Could another person manage them just as effectively, or perhaps even more effectively?

Begin by selecting a single task to assign to someone else. It might involve time-intensive tasks, such as gathering reports or arranging meetings. Clearly communicate your expectations and provide assistance if required. Have you ever received a task with minimal guidance? It's irritating, isn't it? Effective communication guarantees that the individual you delegate to feels prepared to achieve success.

Delegation likewise enhances trust. By demonstrating to your team that you appreciate their abilities, you promote an atmosphere in which they feel motivated to assume responsibility. As time passes, this trust facilitates relinquishing control and concentrating on the tasks that genuinely require your focus.

Have you ever experienced the relief of removing a significant task from your list because another person stepped up? Delegating enables you to concentrate on the larger vision while helping others to develop. It's not about relinquishing your efforts, it's about collaborating more effectively as a team.

Through careful prioritization and effective delegation of tasks, you can take back control of your daily schedule. When you concentrate on what really counts and have a team striving for the same objectives, stress doesn't have to overshadow your plans.

5.3 Building a Support System

As we've discussed, organizing your time can reduce stress, but even the most careful plans can fall apart if you attempt to handle everything alone. No leader, regardless of their experience, achieves success alone. A solid support network, including mentors, friends, and teammates, can be your most valuable asset. But how can you create that network? How can you guarantee that these connections are genuinely beneficial?

Let's begin with mentors. Consider an individual you admire. Perhaps it's a Director who always appeared to have the perfect words to say during difficult times. Or perhaps it's a close friend who has confronted their own difficulties with bravery and insight. An effective mentor doesn't resolve issues on your behalf. They assist you in recognizing opportunities and direct you toward answers. Have you ever found yourself in a position where it seemed every choice was a failure until someone suggested, "How about considering this instead?" That's the type of understanding a mentor provides.

Friends and teammates have distinct roles. These are the individuals you rely on when the burden feels overwhelming. However, relying on others isn't something that feels natural to everyone, is it? Have you ever found yourself wondering, "If I assign this task to someone else, will others perceive me as weak?" It's a frequent concern, yet it lacks basis. Assigning tasks doesn't imply you're avoiding responsibility. It demonstrates that you have confidence in others and appreciate their input. And by doing so, you're not only easing your burden. You're providing chances for others to develop.

Let's dig deeper into how you can find and nurture these connections.

5.3.1 Finding Mentors, Friends, and Teammates to Share the Load

Establishing a support network starts with recognizing the appropriate individuals. Who motivates you? It might be a colleague, a reliable friend, or perhaps a professional you respect from a distance. Avoid overanalyzing your approach to them. An uncomplicated dialogue can make a significant impact. You could express, "I've always respected the way you deal with difficult circumstances. "Are you willing to offer any advice?" Many individuals feel appreciated when asked and are eager to assist.

Regarding friends and teammates, it's important to recognize those you can rely on to support you in times of need. Have you ever felt swamped with tasks and hesitated to seek assistance, thinking, "I don't want to trouble anyone"? In reality, many individuals are happy to help once they understand what's required. Delegating does not equate to offloading responsibilities onto others. It's about distributing responsibility in a manner that advantages all involved. Say, "I'm overwhelmed with this project." Could you manage this task? "It's very significant, and I am sure you would excel at it."

Establishing trust is essential. Relationships flourish when there is mutual respect and effort. Reflect on a moment when a coworker assisted you during a challenging time. What emotions did that evoke in you? Now, reverse the question. When was the most recent occasion you connected with another person? Have you inquired, "How may I assist?" Providing assistance to others enhances your relationships and guarantees they will support you when you need it the most.

Let us not forget the significance of clarity. Have you ever gotten unclear instructions and felt more puzzled than assisted? When you seek assistance, provide details. Rather than stating, "I need this done," consider saying, "Could you check these slides by Friday and tell me if anything requires enhancement?" This method guarantees the task is completed while also making the other individual feel appreciated.

A robust support network is a mutually beneficial relationship. It's about providing as much as you gain. It's about establishing a setting where individuals feel valued, be it through a brief thank-you email or a mention in a team gathering. Such minor acts create loyalty and strengthen the connections that will support you in challenging moments.

However, we shouldn't forget that creating a support system requires time. It's not a thing you can hurry. It requires sincere discussions, common experiences, and consistent effort. Touch base with your mentors. Take time to be with your friends beyond the workplace. Share your challenges and objectives openly with your team. These instances of bonding are what turn casual relationships into trustworthy partnerships.

Keep this in mind, no one achieves success by themselves. By surrounding yourself with individuals who have faith in you, who push you to grow, and who support you, you're doing more than merely alleviating stress. You are evolving into a more resilient, empathetic leader. With mentors to lead you, friends to uplift you, and teammates to experience the journey with, you're creating something much more significant than merely a support system. You are creating a community.

Final Thoughts

Stress is an ever-present factor in leadership, yet it shouldn't determine your approach to leading or your way of life.

This chapter has examined effective tools and methods to assist you in reclaiming control when stress starts to take effect. From soothing your mind through basic exercises to discovering happiness in hobbies and physical pursuits, you've observed how even minor actions can lead to significant changes. Managing your time effectively and establishing priorities means you're optimizing your efforts rather than exhausting yourself, and creating a solid support network reinforces that you're not facing this journey by yourself.

As you think about these strategies, consider which one is the most important? Is it the concept of pausing to inhale before tackling a challenge? Or perhaps considering the idea of relying on a dependable mentor for advice? These tools are not universally applicable. They are designed to fit your specific needs and preferences, helping you develop a sustainable method for handling stress.

Leadership does not mean being flawless in everything we do at work. It revolves around advancement, development, and the capability to adjust. The techniques in this chapter are designed to support you, not confuse you. Begin modestly. Implement one strategy today, whether it's assigning a task, taking a walk, or just contacting someone for assistance. These actions are not solely for handling stress, they represent investments in your health and your capacity to lead with clarity and assurance.

Keep in mind that leadership is not an individual pursuit. With suitable resources, careful preparation, and a nurturing community, you can not only handle stress but also flourish alongside it. Allow these methods to serve as your groundwork as you progress, guiding you with stability and power. You've got this!

06

LEADING WHILE STAYING STRESS-FREE

Leadership involves more than simply achieving results. It concerns the way you guide others as you handle your own stress. Is it possible to instill confidence without feeling overextended? Are you able to stay composed when your team seeks guidance from you? These inquiries are important because leadership entails more than just performance, it requires leaders to be able to balance multiple things.

This chapter emphasizes how you can lead your team while preventing stress from dominating. It examines how establishing clear expectations and collaborating as a team can lessen stress. It also emphasizes the significance of developing a setting in which individuals feel acknowledged, supported, and inspired.

Consider this for a moment. Have you ever encountered a scenario where your team was uncertain because no one understood what was anticipated? Or perhaps deadlines were constantly changing, causing stress and uncertainty for everyone? These are typical challenges, yet they need not determine your leadership. Minor adjustments in communication and organization can lead to significant impacts.

Picture entering a workplace where individuals are motivated, self-assured, and have a clear understanding of their responsibilities. Doesn't that seem like a more favorable place to guide? The positive aspect is that establishing an environment like this is achievable. It begins with how you establish expectations and develop relationships with your team.

In this chapter, we will begin by examining how to establish expectations that all individuals can fulfill. We will explore effective methods to harmonize authority with collaboration, ensuring that no one feels excluded or overwhelmed. Next, we will concentrate on creating a positive work atmosphere, one that promotes open dialogue and recognizes achievements.

Leadership without stress does not imply avoiding difficulties. This involves developing systems and routines that simplify the management of challenges. Regardless of whether you're facing deadlines, resolving conflicts, or commemorating successes, the tactics in this chapter will assist you in leading with confidence and without stress.

6.1 Working with Your Team

Heading a team involves more than simply providing directives. It involves establishing relationships, building trust, and assisting others in achieving success. But how can you achieve that without increasing the burden on yourself?

How can you manage expectations while ensuring the team remains motivated? Such questions frequently occupy the thoughts of leaders, particularly in intense situations.

Consider this. Have you ever provided guidelines only to discover afterward that your team misinterpreted your intentions? Or perhaps you thought everyone understood the steps, but issues arose because the specifics were not obvious. It occurs more frequently than we prefer to acknowledge. The positive aspect is that these circumstances can be prevented through improved communication and organization.

The initial step is establishing clear expectations that all can comprehend. Individuals excel more when they understand precisely what is expected of them. Clarity removes uncertainty and empowers teams to concentrate on completing tasks. However, it doesn't end there. After expectations are established, the following step is to achieve the right balance between guiding and collaborating with your team.

Leadership does not involve being elevated above your team and issuing commands. It focuses on collaborating with them, aiding their initiatives, and being a dependable person for them. Have you ever been employed by someone who made you feel like you belonged to a team? Didn't that inspire you to strive for your best? Consider a moment when you experienced working independently with minimal guidance. Stress escalates rapidly in such scenarios, doesn't it?

This part will assist you in steering clear of those difficulties. We will start by examining how to establish clear expectations that ensure your team remains focused. Next, we will explore methods to balance leadership and collaboration to ensure everyone feels included. Leadership doesn't involve managing every single detail. It involves establishing a framework where each person understands their role and feels appreciated.

Let's begin with our expectations. What is the significance of establishing clear objectives? How can you ensure your team is ready without overseeing every detail? How can you modify your approach when situations don't unfold as expected? These are inquiries that every leader encounters, and the responses can alter your leadership approach.

6.1.1 Setting Clear Expectations Everyone Can Meet

Clarity is among the most powerful tools that a leader can employ. Have you ever entered a meeting and departed, unsure of what precisely needed to be accomplished? Or assigned tasks to your group only to find out later that nobody grasped the priorities? It occurs more frequently than we realize. Misunderstandings lead to delays, and delays lead to stress. Yet, what if this could be prevented?

Establishing expectations goes beyond merely assigning tasks. It's about ensuring that all are aware of what success entails. Picture requesting an individual to coordinate a project. Are they aware of the due date? Are they aware of the expectations you have for standards? Or are they making assumptions and wishing they were doing it correctly? Lacking details, even the most talented team can feel directionless.

Begin with the fundamentals. What actions must be taken? Who holds accountability for each section? When is the deadline? Record it or verbalize it. Clarity eliminates uncertainty and provides individuals with a distinct goal. It also aids in their concentration. Consider the contrast between entering a dimly lit room and stepping into a brightly illuminated space. Transparent expectations illuminate the path.

However, what happens when plans shift? What happens if priorities change in the middle? That's where consistent check-ins play a role. Rather than waiting until the conclusion to observe outcomes, arrange brief updates. Inquire with phrases such as, "How is everything progressing?" or "Is there any confusion?" These brief discussions assist in identifying issues promptly before they escalate into larger problems.

And how about feedback? Individuals must understand where they stand. Have you ever experienced doubt regarding your ability to meet expectations? It's quite stressful, isn't it? This is the reason feedback is important. It maintains your team's confidence and concentration. Commend their advancement. Identify areas that require correction. However, always clarify what is functioning and what is not.

Clarity involves more than just language. It's also concerned with tone and timing. Picture providing someone with last-minute guidance just before a due date. What would that sensation be like? Rather, allow individuals ample time to understand what is anticipated. Inquire if they require further explanation. Inquiries such as "Does this add up?" or "What will you do next?" can indicate if everyone understands the situation similarly.

When expectations are clearly identified, individuals feel prepared to take action. They invest less time in pondering and more time in acting. When they achieve success, it builds confidence, not only in their skills but also in you as their leader.

6.1.2 Balancing Leadership with Teamwork to Reduce Tension

Leadership frequently brings the expectation of possessing all the solutions. However, here's the reality. Leaders don't need to handle everything. Have you ever felt that you needed to manage everything on your own because seeking assistance could make you appear vulnerable? Numerous leaders think this, but it's just not correct. Effective leaders do not bear the burden by themselves. They understand how to manage leading while collaborating with their teams.

Reflect on your personal experiences. Have you ever had a boss who seemed detached, issuing commands without genuine engagement? Or perhaps you experienced a leader who immersed themselves in every detail, allowing no space for others to participate. Both methods are ineffective. The most effective teams function optimally when leaders understand when to intervene and when to refrain.

Begin by questioning yourself, "What does my team require from me at this moment?" Occasionally, they require guidance. At other moments, they simply require assistance. There are times when they require some space to sort things out on their own. Understanding when to alternate between these roles can alleviate the stress for both you and your team.

For instance, imagine a strict deadline. Your group is striving to complete a project, and anxiety levels are increasing. Do you intervene and take charge, or do you inquire, "How can I assist?" Straightforward inquiries like this demonstrate your engagement without asserting dominance. It also assists you in identifying areas where the team may require additional support.

Balance also signifies being present without interfering. Have you ever collaborated with someone who checked in so frequently it seemed disruptive? Micromanagement can generate stress and hinder the advancement of talented individuals. Rather, establish consistent times to monitor tasks and have faith in your team to manage the remainder. If they are aware of your presence when required, they will feel more assured in handling their duties.

Dividing responsibilities also helps teamwork feel effortless. Have you ever observed how a team's motivation changes when leaders participate? Even minor acts, such as remaining late to assist with a report or volunteering to take on part of a task, can inspire others to perform at their best. It demonstrates that leadership involves collaboration rather than mere control.

Mitigating stress doesn't imply completely eliminating pressure. It's about developing a setting where pressure doesn't hinder efficiency. Teams that feel encouraged are more prone to tackle difficulties without losing concentration.

A simple method to reduce stress is by engaging in conversations. When did you last inquire with your team, "What's going well for you?" or "Is there anything that complicates this process more than necessary?" These inquiries may uncover concealed issues and develop trust. They also indicate to your team that you appreciate their contributions.

Combining leadership with collaboration produces more than just outcomes. It creates an environment in which individuals feel secure, encouraged, and inspired. When each person understands their role and feels appreciated, stress lessens, and productivity goes up.

Let's progress and explore how establishing a healthy workplace can enhance these concepts even further.

6.2 Creating a Healthy Working Environment

Leaders establish the atmosphere for their teams, and the ambiance they foster can either enhance productivity or cultivate frustration. A work environment in which individuals feel valued, secure, and inspired doesn't occur by chance. It requires effort, clear intentions, and continuous adjustments. How can you establish that type of environment? What actions can you implement to ensure your team remains connected, assured, and motivated?

A healthy workplace isn't focused on achieving perfection. It revolves around establishing trust and maintaining open channels of communication. Individuals need to feel that their voices are acknowledged and that their contributions are significant. They ought to feel at ease to express ideas, voice concerns, and celebrate successes freely. When this occurs, teams perform more effectively. Errors transform into opportunities for growth, and difficulties become simpler to handle.

However, let's be truthful. Establishing this type of atmosphere isn't always simple. Deadlines accumulate, priorities change, and stress begins to rise. This is why leaders must be deliberate in promoting habits that sustain high morale. Minor deeds frequently have the greatest impact. A simple "thank you" for a task completed effectively, a brief team gathering to touch base, or just inquiring, "How are you?" can make a significant difference.

The aim here isn't solely to enhance performance. The aim is to establish an environment where individuals feel appreciated and backed, even during challenging times at work. A team that feels valued is more prone to remain motivated and less likely to break down under stress.

So, how do you make this happen? It starts with two things, communication and recognition. These aren't just fancy leadership terms. They're tools that help people feel connected and give them a reason to stay committed. Let's look closer at how they can transform your workplace.

6.2.1 Encouraging Open Communication and Recognition of Successes

Have you ever attended a meeting where the team members are reluctant to participate? Or participated in a project where feedback arrived too late to correct errors?

Ineffective communication can lead to greater issues than the difficulties you initially aimed to address. That's the reason encouraging open discussions is so important. But what does that actually appear to be?

It begins by ensuring that individuals feel secure in expressing themselves. Have you ever requested thoughts and received nothing in response? It occurs more frequently than you might expect. Individuals occasionally refrain from speaking up due to a fear of being incorrect or offending others. As a leader, it is your responsibility to dispel that fear.

Give this a go the next time you find yourself in a meeting. Instead of saying, "Any thoughts?" you might say, "I'm eager to know your view on this." "What do you believe we should prioritize initially?" A slight change in phrasing can encourage individuals to feel more at ease when expressing their thoughts. When they express themselves, they should ensure they understand that their contributions are appreciated. A brief "That's an excellent point" or "I appreciate you mentioning that" promotes increased involvement.

Hearing is also a significant aspect of communication. Have you ever sensed that someone wasn't genuinely listening when you talked? It's annoying, isn't it? Now turn that inside out. When a team member engages with you, demonstrate that you are completely attentively listening. Set aside your phone, keep eye contact, and restate what you heard to ensure you grasped their message. These minor gestures demonstrate that their words hold significance, thereby building trust.

However, communication shouldn't be limited to times when there's an issue to resolve. Frequent check-ins assist in ensuring that everyone is coordinated and aware of priorities. They also provide chances to address minor problems before they escalate into larger ones. These discussions don't need to be official. At times, a brief conversation during a coffee break can be equally as effective as a planned meeting.

Now, let's discuss acknowledgment. Have you ever put in effort on something and felt like nobody recognized it? It's quite discouraging, isn't it? This is why it is crucial to celebrate victories, both significant and minor. Individuals should be aware that their contributions are valued. And no, acknowledgment doesn't necessarily need to be given as a bonus or a reward. A straightforward "Great job" can brighten someone's whole day.

How frequently do you set aside time to recognize your team's efforts? If you have doubts, it could be the right moment to establish that habit. Begin by specifying the praise. Rather than simply saying, "Good job," highlight the specific aspects that impressed you. Consider, "I truly appreciated the way you managed that client call." "Your readiness was evident, and it had an impact." When individuals are aware of what they excel at, they are more inclined to replicate it.

Team celebrations are excellent for creating positivity and excitement in the organization. Did your group complete an important project? Introduce coffee and pastries to celebrate the event. Did anyone exceed expectations? Acknowledge them briefly in your upcoming team meeting. These minor actions serve to remind individuals that their contributions are important, and this feeling of significance can enhance performance.

Recognition isn't solely a top-down process. Motivate team members to complement one another. Recognition from peers can be as significant as receiving compliments from a manager. Basic tools, such as a communal gratitude board or weekly acknowledgments, can simplify this process.

When communication is smooth and acknowledgment appears authentic, the workplace transforms. Individuals begin to exchange ideas with greater openness. They are inspired to perform at their highest level since they understand it's recognized. Conflicts lessen, and cooperation is enhanced. It's not solely about completing the task. It's about building an environment where individuals feel motivated and honored to participate.

Ultimately, a positive workplace is founded on trust, respect, and gratitude. When teams experience a sense of connection and support, stress does not dominate. Rather, individuals confront obstacles and collaborate to discover answers. Isn't that the essence of exceptional leadership?

Final Thoughts

Recognition isn't solely a top-down process. Motivate team members to complement one another. Recognition from peers can be as significant as receiving compliments from a manager. Basic tools, such as a communal gratitude board or weekly acknowledgments, can simplify this process.

When communication is smooth and acknowledgment appears authentic, the workplace transforms positively. Individuals begin to exchange ideas with greater openness. They are inspired to perform at their highest level since they understand it's recognized. Conflicts lessen, and cooperation is enhanced. It's not solely about completing the task. It's about building an environment where individuals feel motivated and honored to participate.

Ultimately, a positive workplace is founded on trust, respect, and gratitude. When teams experience a sense of connection and support, stress does not dominate. Rather, individuals confront obstacles and collaborate to discover answers. Isn't that the essence of exceptional leadership? Let's see how.

07

BALANCING WORK AND PERSONAL LIFE

Leadership often feels like juggling too many balls at once. Deadlines, meetings, and emails occupy the day, providing scant time for other activities. Before you realize it, personal time vanishes, and the equilibrium between work and life begins to fade. Does that ring a bell? If that's the case, you're in good company.

In the previous chapters, we examined methods to handle stress, enhance resilience, and lead without experiencing burnout. We discussed identifying triggers, preparing in advance, maintaining composure, and looking for encouraging settings. The emphasis was on managing stress successfully to prevent it from dominating your life. However, how do you safeguard your personal time? This section provides an answer to that inquiry.

Let's speak frankly. Work can occupy more space than necessary. It frequently begins with a brief email post-dinner or reviewing messages while at a family event. Soon, it turns into a routine, and personal time is sidelined. Must it be that manner? Not in the slightest. Leadership doesn't require giving up your nights, weekends, or personal health. The most effective leaders understand how to protect their time and prioritize what is most important.

This chapter does not focus on avoiding responsibilities. It's about establishing clear boundaries and maintaining them. It's about using your personal time for activities that invigorate you and discovering methods to remain refreshed, ensuring you perform your best at both work and home.

We'll start with setting limits and creating boundaries that protect your personal space. After that, we'll look at making time for activities that recharge you. We'll wrap up with simple ways to keep your mind and body feeling strong and rested.

You're here because you want balance, not burnout. Balance isn't just nice to have. It's necessary if you want to lead effectively without losing yourself in the process. Let's see how you can make it happen.

7.1 Setting Limits to Protect Your Personal Time

How often do you find yourself saying, "Just one more email," or, "I'll finish this and then stop"? It sounds harmless, yet before you know it, an hour has slipped away, and your night is lost. It's simple to get caught in this situation, particularly when tasks seem pressing. But when does it conclude? And even more crucially, at what price?

Establishing boundaries isn't about excluding work entirely. It's about determining where work concludes and personal time starts. Consider it as shutting the door to your workspace when the day concludes. When that door is closed, the work remains within. Is it always perceived as simple? No. However, establishing that boundary is what prevents your personal life from turning into an extension of the workplace.

Here's an illustration. Rose, who works as a general manager, typically kept her phone beside her bed. She would look at emails late at night and first thing in the morning. Initially, it appeared to be effective. However, as time passed, she realized she was always feeling exhausted. Even when she wasn't on duty, her thoughts remained focused on the office. Does this ring a bell?

One evening, Rose chose to silence her phone without any notification. Initially, it felt odd. She feared she could overlook something significant. However, nothing occurred. Rather, she had improved sleep and awoke feeling more refreshed. She understood that many emails could be postponed until morning, and the company didn't collapse just because she didn't reply immediately.

You don't need to completely isolate yourself. Minor adjustments can lead to significant impact. Consider establishing a specific end time each day. Shut your laptop, mute notifications, and inform your team about when you'll be reachable again. When you communicate clearly about your off-work hours, others are more prone to value your time.

Boundaries function more effectively when they remain consistent. If you look at emails one evening while having dinner and overlook them the next, it creates confusion.

Individuals will be uncertain about what to anticipate. It's like keeping the door open and questioning why others disregard your boundaries. However, when your boundaries remain consistent, others start to respect them.

If a person rings you at 10 p.m. for non-emergency matter and you answer, you are signaling to them that calls at that hour are acceptable. However, if you allow it to go to voicemail and call back the following morning, you are establishing a different expectation. It's not about being inaccessible. It's important to be specific regarding your availability.

One more useful tip is to keep work and personal devices apart. If feasible, have one phone designated for work and another for personal purposes. Once the workday concludes, power down the work phone and keep it out of reach. Making this minor change can enhance mental clarity and strengthen the separation between your work and personal time.

What is effective for one individual may not be effective for someone else. Perhaps you should set aside one evening each week for family time. Or perhaps weekends should be entirely free of work. The important aspect is to understand how balance appears for you and then adhere to it.

It equally aids in having open communication with your team. Inform them of your unavailability and motivate them to reciprocate. Creating a culture that values personal time can relieve some of your stress and encourage others to feel more at ease in establishing their own limits.

Here are a few simple tips to help you set limits and stick to them:

- Use an auto-responder to let people know when you'll be available.

- Schedule downtime on your calendar, just like meetings, so it doesn't get overlooked.

- Create physical boundaries, like a dedicated workspace, and step away from it once your work hours end.

- Set daily goals and stop working once they're done instead of pushing for more.

- Keep work apps off your personal phone to avoid unnecessary interruptions.

Protecting your time isn't selfish. It's what allows you to recharge so you can show up fully when you are working. When you set limits, you're not just creating space for yourself. You're also showing others that it's okay to do the same.

So, where can you start? Look at your week and decide where you need stronger boundaries. Make one small change today. Turn off notifications after dinner. Block time in your calendar for yourself. Close your laptop when your work hours end. Take note of how it feels when you stick to those limits. The difference might surprise you.

7.2 Making Time for Activities That Energize You

Once you've set boundaries around your personal time, what do you do with it? That's the next step. It's not solely about making space. It's about using that time for activities that make you feel invigorated and inspired.

Reflect on the most recent occasion when you engaged in an activity that you truly loved. Perhaps it was a leisurely walk along the beach, being engaged in your sports activity, or enjoying moments with companions. How did it make you feel? Did you sense a feeling of lightness? More concentrated? More content? Those instances aren't merely pleasant to experience. They are essential.

Leaders frequently become so focused on productivity that they overlook the importance of engaging in activities that bring them happiness. Spending time on what you enjoy is not a waste of time. It's about putting resources into yourself to improve your presence when it counts the most.

What motivates you may differ from what motivates another person. It might be jogging, creating art, playing an instrument, or just sitting quietly with a cup of nice coffee. The activity is less important than the emotions it evokes in you. The crucial aspect is to make it a priority.

But how can you find a time when your timetable seems full? Begin with small steps. Set aside 20 minutes for yourself and consider it as significant as any other crucial meeting. Mark it on your calendar to ensure it doesn't get overlooked. Make the most of this time by engaging in something meaningful, whether it's just going outside for some fresh air or looking through a beloved book.

Consider trying out different morning routines. What if your day began with something that energizes you? It might involve stretching, writing in a journal, or listening to music. Such minor rituals can establish the mood for an improved day. If mornings are overly hectic, look for a moment later in the evening when things settle down.

A different strategy is to integrate energizing activities with current obligations. For instance, enjoy reading your favorite book while traveling or taking a short distance walk during lunch hours. Just a few minutes of engaging in an activity you love can make you feel revitalized.

Do not overlook the significance of diversity. Engaging in the same activity daily can occasionally turn it into just another item on your list of things to do. Switch among various hobbies to maintain variety. Perhaps Monday is designated for sports, Tuesday for hanging around with friends, and Wednesday for a brisk workout at the gym. Mixing things up can maintain your energy levels.

If you struggle to put yourself first, pose this question. Would you advise another person to take breaks and engage in hobbies? If the response is affirmative, then what stops you from doing the same for yourself? Caring for your energy not only helps yourself. It assists all those who rely on you.

It also aids in creating an atmosphere that feels positive, healthy and full of energy. Is there a spot in your house where you can relax and take it easy? A tiny corner with a chair and proper lighting can turn into your favorite place for relaxation. The environment is more important than you realize.

Compile a roster of activities that bring you joy. Keep it close and consult it whenever you find some free time. This way, you won't spend time figuring out what to do.

Incorporate a combination of brief five-minute tasks and extended activities that can occupy an hour. The aim is to incorporate energizing activities as a routine habit rather than something you fit in when there's spare time.

Finally, include others whenever possible. Participating in activities with friends or family can enhance their enjoyment. Organize a weekend trek, participate in a book club, or ask someone to explore a new hobby alongside you. Including others in the experience makes it simpler to remain consistent and motivated.

It's simple to allow the day to pass by without dedicating some moments to yourself, yet minor adjustments can assist you in taking back that time. Begin by selecting one activity for this week that energizes you, and ensure it is non-negotiable. Once it's on your calendar, regard it with the same significance as any other appointment. You will be amazed at how much your mood has improved when you consistently replenish your energy.

7.3 Finding Ways to Refresh Your Mind and Body Regularly

Setting aside time for activities that make you happy and free your mind is a wonderful beginning, but it's just as crucial to emphasize routines that regularly rejuvenate both your mind and body. It's not solely about pauses. It's about establishing routines that help you feel centered, focused, and physically robust.

Have you ever experienced such mental exhaustion that a restful night's sleep didn't make a difference? That indicates your mind requires more than mere rest. It requires deliberate attention. Practices such as meditation, deep breathing exercises, and journaling can soothe hurried thoughts and enhance concentration. Just ten minutes of peaceful contemplation can create an impact.

Consider Alia as an illustration. She would begin her mornings hurriedly, checking messages and emails as she ate her breakfast. As time passed, she sensed that her thoughts were constantly in motion, exhausting her before the day even started. One morning, Alia chose to alter her daily routine. Rather than grabbing her phone, she went out to her garden and took ten minutes to relish the refreshing morning air while sipping a cup of tea. She observed the birds singing and felt the soft wind against her face. Within a few days, she noticed how much more peaceful her mornings had turned. She experienced greater control, her concentration enhanced, and she started anticipating this minor yet revitalizing routine every day.

Your body requires care as well. Being physically active doesn't necessarily require strenuous exercise. A quick walk, gardening, or even gentle stretching can relieve stress and elevate your spirits. Consider it as providing your body the refresh it requires to continue thriving.

Revitalizing your mind and body doesn't always require significant shifts. Occasionally, it's the tiniest changes that create the most significant impact. If you sit for extended periods, taking frequent breaks to get up and move can quickly boost your energy levels. Rising, stretching, or simply walking to get more water can help keep your body engaged and avoid stiffness. Basic desk movements such as shoulder rolls or neck stretches can aid in relieving tension, particularly if your job requires extended periods in front of a computer.

In addition to exercise, fresh air can greatly enhance your mood and concentration. Step outside for a little while, bask in the sunlight and allow your mind to unwind. A relaxing walk around the office blocks can refresh your mind and provide the reset necessary to tackle tasks with improved concentration.

Breathing drills provide a rapid method to refresh. Taking deep breaths soothes your nervous system and lowers stress levels. Attempt to inhale gently through your nose, pause for several seconds, and then exhale through your mouth. Doing this several times throughout the day can help you feel grounded and more in command.

Don't underestimate the importance of hydration. Consuming sufficient water during the day can maintain your energy levels and avoid tiredness. Place a water bottle on your desk to prompt you to drink often. Incorporate this with brief pauses, and you'll discover that you feel more revitalized without disrupting your work process.

Small modifications can accumulate. Increasing water intake, taking breaks from screens, or enjoying nature can refresh your mind and boost your energy. The aim is to develop routines that maintain your sense of balance, not merely at times but daily.

If you're curious about incorporating these habits into your routine, begin by linking them with activities you already engage in. Do some stretching while your coffee is brewing. Play your favorite music while you cook dinner.

Take a walk during phone meetings if you don't need to jot things down. It's about incorporating brief moments of revitalization into your current routine so that it doesn't come across as an additional chore.

You can also engage others to simplify the process. Consider a brief exercise practice with your family or enjoy walking with a colleague at lunchtime. Participating in these activities together can enhance their enjoyment and assist you in maintaining consistency.

Another suggestion is to set up reminders to refocus your attention during the day. Set an alarm every two hours to wake up and practice deep breathing. Put sticky notes on your desk with prompts like, "Stay hydrated" or "Take a stretch break." Small reminders can help you stick to these habits until they feel automatic.

Make sure to include moments of play throughout your day. Participating in activities like dancing to a favorite song, enjoying a fun hobby, or playing a short game can uplift your mood and refresh your mind. Ultimately, laughter is among the most powerful methods to reduce stress.

In the end, do not overlook the importance of sleep. Getting adequate rest is one of the best ways to refresh both your body and mind. Create a nightly routine that signals to your body it's time to unwind. Avoid screens for an hour before bed, read a book, or practice gratitude by jotting down some positive thoughts from your day.

To go further, think about weekly resets. Set aside one evening or weekend morning to fully disconnect, no emails, no social media, merely time to relax. You might visit a local park, experiment with a different recipe, or just unwind with a beloved film. These extended breaks provide your body and mind with a more profound refreshment.

Caring for your body and mind isn't a luxury. It's an essential requirement. By incorporating these habits into your life, you'll experience increased presence, improved focus, and greater control. Begin with one or two adjustments and observe their impact on your energy levels. The aim isn't flawlessness, it's reliability.

Final Thoughts

Achieving a balance between work and personal life involves more than simply organizing your schedule. It involves making intentional decisions that help you safeguard your time, rejuvenate your energy, and be present entirely for both your job and personal life. Establishing limits, focusing on actions that invigorate you, and incorporating routines that rejuvenate your mind and body are not optional, they're essential.

As seen in this chapter, incremental actions can result in significant transformations. Whether it involves disabling notifications post-work, going for a walk at lunchtime, or enjoying moments with family, these practices support you in remaining centered and preventing burnout. The objective isn't to remove stress completely. It's about handling it in ways that promote your well-being and leadership.

But what happens when stress builds up despite your efforts? That's what we will look at in the next chapter. We'll take a closer look at common mistakes leaders make when they're feeling stressed. From trying to handle everything alone to ignoring burnout signs, we'll explore practical ways to avoid these pitfalls and maintain balance even during the most demanding times. Let's continue building the skills you need to lead with confidence and clarity.

08

AVOIDING COMMON MISTAKES WHEN FEELING STRESSED

In the previous chapter, we discussed achieving balance, establishing boundaries, allocating time for activities that rejuvenate you, and revitalizing your mind and body to lead without exhaustion. But what occurs when stress creeps in regardless? What if, even with your utmost attempts, the stress begins to accumulate?

Stress tends to accumulate silently. Initially, it's controllable. An overlooked deadline here. An email sent late at night. Before you realize it, you're spread too thin and attempting to keep everything intact. And when that occurs, it's simple to slip into behaviors that worsen the situation rather than improve it.

Have you ever found yourself contemplating, "I really need to manage this alone," or "If I put just a bit more effort, everything will align perfectly"? It seems like the correct decision at this time. However, later on, you feel exhausted, anxious, and uncertain about how you arrived at that point.

The reality is that stress isn't the enemy. What truly counts is our reaction to it. This chapter discusses identifying the typical errors leaders commit when under stress and effective strategies to prevent these missteps.

We'll start by looking at one of the most common mistakes, trying to handle everything yourself.

8.1 Trying to Handle Everything on Your Own

Have you ever felt, "If I don't take care of this, it won't be done properly"? It's a belief shared by numerous leaders, and it frequently seems warranted. Ultimately, you are accountable for the outcomes. However, attempting to manage every issue on your own can lead to swift consequences.

When I was the CEO of my telecommunication company, I encountered a unique challenge. As a chartered accountant by profession, running a highly technical business meant relying on my team for expertise in areas I wasn't fully familiar with. Delegating tasks to the technical team wasn't always easy, especially when I noticed gaps in their communication and human interaction skills. In the beginning, this created a lot of stress related to relationships with customers. The team excelled in their technical work, but when it came to dealing with customers or higher management, things didn't flow smoothly. Meetings were often unorganized, and customer relationships lacked the warmth and understanding needed to build trust. I found myself stepping in far too often, wondering how to bridge this gap without taking on more than I could handle. That's when I realized the solution wasn't to take over their tasks but to help them improve in areas where they struggled. Drawing from my experience as a corporate and leadership trainer, I designed a soft skills program specifically for the technical team. The program focused on guiding them on how to communicate effectively with customers, work smoothly with management, and able to close projects efficiently.

The transformation was incredible. After completing the program and gaining hands-on experience, the team became more confident and capable. They managed projects from start to finish, secured final acceptance tests, and closed contracts on time. Customers started building stronger relationships with the company, and I no longer felt the need to intervene at every step. Delegation became less of a task and more of a natural process because I trusted their abilities. For me, the main lesson was straightforward. Each team has its own advantages and disadvantages, and it's better to work with them than against them. In this process, delegation was essential. I wasn't simply relieving my own stress when I trusted my team with tasks and provided them with the resources they required to be successful. I was boosting their self-esteem, honing their abilities, and establishing an atmosphere where everyone could thrive together. Delegation is about working together to improve results for the team and the organization, not about giving up control.

When was the last time you asked for help? Did you find it simple, or did you pause, concerned it could portray you as vulnerable? Leaders frequently worry that seeking assistance could tarnish their image. However, the reverse is accurate. Assigning tasks does not indicate a lack of strength. It demonstrates confidence.

Throughout the Apollo 11 lunar landing, flight director Gene Kranz encountered one of the most intense situations ever recorded. He directed the mission control team that assisted Neil Armstrong and Buzz Aldrin during their landmark expedition. Kranz did not try to make every decision on his own. Rather, he enabled his team to oversee systems, resolve issues, and make essential decisions. His capability to rely on his team and assign responsibilities enabled him to concentrate on ensuring the mission's success instead of micromanaging every aspect. The outcome was one of the most renowned accomplishments in human history.

Kranz's method serves as a reminder that leadership isn't about handling everything by oneself. This means establishing a setting where people can assume responsibility, share their skills, and collaborate toward a common objective. Leaders who rely on their teams not only reduce their own stress but also build trust and abilities in others. If you've ever had the impulse to handle everything on your own, consider this. What could occur if you allowed another person to take charge of a specific task? What's the best that could occur? Frequently, you'll discover that allowing others to help carry the burden simplifies matters for all involved.

In the next section, we'll look at another common mistake, ignoring the signs of burnout or overwork.

8.2 Ignoring the Signs of Burnout or Overwork

Leaders frequently overlook burnout, believing it to be merely an aspect of the job. They continue to push, believing that the feeling of being tired or irritated will fade. However, burnout does not resolve itself independently. It accumulates, impacting concentration, choices, and well-being. Gradually, it erodes motivation and may result in physical health problems, complicating recovery.

Identifying burnout early can help you avoid larger issues down the line. Be aware of your body and emotions. Feeling exhausted even after taking a break? Losing your patience fast? Having difficulty concentrating? These are warning signs. Disregarding them doesn't enhance your strength. It complicates the process of recovery.

Begin with limitations. Establish defined working hours and adhere to them. If possible, avoid checking emails late at night or during your breaks. Allocate proper time for eating and brief strolls. Minor activities such as taking a break from your workstation or inhaling deeply for several minutes can refresh your mind and body.

Monitor your workload consistently. Consider whether you are overextending yourself. Be truthful about whether you are managing your priorities effectively or just agreeing to all requests. Divide large tasks into smaller, manageable steps. Assigning tasks isn't a flaw. It's a method to maintain productivity and avoid feeling tired.

Create habits that assist you in relaxing after work. Whether it's taking a brisk walk, enjoying your favorite sport, or being with family, establish routines that distinguish work from leisure time. Regard this downtime as essential and non-negotiable, similar to any significant meeting.

Incorporate mental resets throughout your day. Spend five minutes jotting down your thoughts. This can assist you in clearing disorganized thoughts and regaining focus. Reach out to a trusted person when burdens weigh you down. Don't bear the burden by yourself. Cultivate gratitude by noting three positive events that occurred at the conclusion of each day. This straightforward task can redirect your attention from stress to advancement.

An additional useful habit is to establish achievable objectives for each day. Rather than attempting to achieve everything simultaneously, select a handful of essential tasks to concentrate on. Acknowledge little victories, no matter how insignificant they may appear. Advancement is encouraging and contributes to preventing burnout.

Ultimately, take time to reflect on yourself weekly. Inquire, "What's one thing I can release?" or "What's one habit I can incorporate to achieve more balance?" Assess your tasks and priorities. Do you notice any trends where you overcommit yourself? Modify as necessary. These minor adjustments can prevent burnout from the beginning and help you remain steady as a leader.

Up next, we'll explore another mistake that often goes unnoticed, expecting too much from yourself and those around you without realizing the strain it creates.

8.3 Pushing Yourself and Others Too Hard Without Realizing It and Beyond Capacity

When stress accumulates, it's simple to fall into the pattern of pushing more, both yourself and those nearby. It frequently begins with positive motives. You aim to meet deadlines, achieve outcomes, and maintain progress. However, without awareness, the rhythm turns unmanageable, resulting in everyone feeling exhausted and uninspired.

Constantly pushing yourself to overperform will cause a chain reaction. When leaders drive themselves to the edge, they unknowingly create unachievable standards for their teams. Workers might sense a duty to reciprocate that enthusiasm, even if it's more than they can handle. This may result in bitterness, diminished performance, and increased turnover. Rather than inspiring others, too much pressure can lead individuals to feel unappreciated and stressed.

Another danger of pushing too hard is the breakdown of trust. When people are constantly under pressure, mistakes happen. Leaders who respond to mistakes with frustration rather than support risk creating a culture of fear. Instead of focusing on solutions, teams may start hiding errors to avoid criticism, which only compounds problems.

Leaders also risk losing creativity and innovation when pressure is too high. Teams focused solely on meeting deadlines often miss opportunities to think outside the box or experiment with new ideas. Over time, this limits growth as well as potential.

To avoid these pitfalls, leaders must recognize the signs of pushing too hard. Are deadlines constantly being missed? Are meetings filled with tension? Is turnover increasing? These are signals that workloads may be unrealistic and that adjustments are needed.

Rather than pushing harder, leaders ought to encourage balance. Begin by establishing achievable deadlines and dividing extensive projects into smaller, manageable tasks. Inspire team members to express worries about their workloads openly, free from fear of criticism. Offer tools and resources to simplify tasks and recognize progress rather than concentrating solely on the end goal.

It's equally important to develop healthy habits. Take pauses, depart from work on schedule, and inspire others to follow suit. Demonstrate to your team that outcomes are important, but so is well-being. Consistently reach out to people to assess their stress levels and inquire about how you can assist.

Realistic modifications can create a significant impact. Incorporate buffer time into schedules to prevent urgent tasks from interfering with other responsibilities. Promote adaptable work hours whenever feasible. Consistently touch base with team members, focusing not only on progress but also on their emotions. Occasionally, a brief conversation about their difficulties can result in straightforward answers that lighten stress.

Finally, reflect on long-term goals. Sustainable success isn't about pushing through every roadblock at full speed. It's about creating systems that allow for steady progress. Celebrate small wins and recognize when adjustments are needed.

With this chapter, we've explored three common mistakes leaders make when stressed, handling everything alone, ignoring burnout, and pushing too hard. The good news is that these patterns can be changed. It starts with awareness and small adjustments that keep you and your team strong, focused, and energized. When you lead with balance, you don't just meet goals, you create an environment where everyone can thrive.

Final Thoughts

Leadership brings its own set of challenges, and how you respond to stress can influence whether you succeed or feel swamped. Your attitude influences not only your own wellness but also the performance and spirit of your team. This chapter explored three typical mistakes, attempting to handle everything alone, overlooking burnout, and exerting excessive pressure. These patterns frequently remain unnoticed until they inflict significant harm.

Awareness is the first step to breaking these habits. Leaders who master delegation foster trust and empower their teams. Noticing signs of burnout helps to tackle issues early on before they escalate. Stepping back to assess workloads and expectations avoids burnout and sustains creativity.

Sustainable leadership does not mean the leader is compromising their capability. It involves guiding in a manner that fosters consistent development without sacrificing well-being. Minor adjustments in strategy, such as seeking assistance, establishing limits, and valuing rest, can create a significant effect.

When leaders prioritize balance, they foster settings where teams feel encouraged, inspired, and prepared to excel at their highest level. Stress may not vanish, but adopting the right mindset and habits can make it manageable, creating space for clarity, confidence, and lasting success.

09

BUILDING HABITS THAT KEEP STRESS AWAY

Stress doesn't just show up when deadlines are tight or problems pile up. It often sneaks in quietly through daily routines. Numerous late nights, missed meals, and never-ending to-do lists can turn stress into an unwelcome visitor that won't go away. The previous chapter emphasized how common errors, such as attempting to manage everything alone or overlooking burnout, can increase stress. However, even after you identify these patterns, what follows? What methods can you use to prevent stress from returning? That's the point at which habits can have an impact.

Consider the routines you currently follow. Perhaps you look at emails first thing in the morning or check your phone just before going to sleep. These activities may appear useless, yet they influence your day more than you think. What if you could swap some of those habits for ones that truly simplify life? Minor adjustments, such as taking a moment to breathe before a meeting or allocating five minutes to organize your day, can create a significant impact. This chapter focuses on creating habits that not only handle stress but also keep it away. It is about starting small and staying consistent so these habits stick. No big leaps. No drastic changes. Just simple steps that fit into your routine.

We will look at how starting with easy, achievable tasks can set the tone for stress-free days. We will talk about reflecting on what is working and making tweaks when something is not. And we will explore ways to inspire your team to focus on healthier ways of working. After all, stress-free leadership is not just about you. It is about creating an example others can follow. By the end of this chapter, you will see how steady, thoughtful actions can shift the way you approach stress. Whether you are leading a team or managing your own workload, these habits will help you stay grounded and ready for whatever comes next. Let's get started.

9.1 Staying Consistent with Small, Achievable Tasks and Daily Actions

Stress frequently appears more significant than it truly is because we attempt to handle everything simultaneously. It's simple to believe, "I'll sort everything out today," but major objectives lacking a strategy can swiftly result in disappointment. In reality, significant transformation arises from minor deeds practiced consistently each day. Consider beginning your day with one easy success. It might involve tidying your bed, having a glass of water, or jotting down three things to do today. Minor victories create momentum. When the situation is unpredictable and when we are unsure whether or not we will be able to achieve our targets, such minor victories will serve as reminders to our minds that progress is achievable.

When tasks feel like they are too big and difficult to manage, dividing them into smaller steps can help make them more manageable. Rather than attempting to tidy up your whole desk, focus on just one drawer. If your inbox seems overwhelming, concentrate on replying to five emails before proceeding to another task. Minor successes propel you onward without leaving you exhausted. It helps in establishing practical expectations. Individuals frequently believe that productivity equates to accomplishing as much as possible, yet it actually revolves around concentrating on what is most important. Jot down one or two main tasks for the day rather than burdening yourself with an extensive list. Marking off just one significant task can give you a sense of achievement.

If beginning seems difficult, concentrate on the tiniest step you can make. Perhaps it's organizing a single folder in your inbox or cleaning up your desk before concluding the day. These small actions will give you a feeling of control and prepare your mind for larger tasks. Establishing habits becomes simpler when you link them to activities you already engage in. If you have tea each morning, take those moments to outline your tasks for the day. If you look at your calendar in the afternoon, take that opportunity to reflect on what succeeded and what can be better for tomorrow. When habits seamlessly blend into your daily life, they seem less like a task and more like an integral aspect of your routine.

Notifications can be useful as well. Place a sticky note on your desk featuring an encouraging message, such as "Concentrate on one step today." Alternatively, configure a phone alarm named "Take a break and breathe." Basic nudges like these facilitate the maintenance of new habits, even during hectic schedules. Visual tracking tools can also help maintain habits. Consider utilizing a calendar to indicate each day you successfully maintain your habit. Observing your advancement increases motivation. Certain individuals discover it beneficial to maintain a habit journal to note their achievements and difficulties. Recording information strengthens dedication.

It's essential to understand that consistency does not equate to perfection. On certain days, events may not unfold as expected. That's okay. What is important is to regain focus rather than becoming disheartened. Achievement arises from being present, even if only for a short time. Everyday activities, regardless of their size, accumulate. As time goes on, they gain confidence, lessen stress, and turn large goals into achievable tasks. Honor each progress made, no matter how small. Soon enough, those habits will seem second nature, and there will be less space for stress to take hold.

9.2 Reflecting on What Works for You and Adjusting as Needed

Building habits is not just about sticking to routines. It is also about knowing when to pause and ask, "Is this still working for me?" Sometimes, what seems effective at first can lose its impact over time. That is why reflection matters. It helps you stay aware of what is helping and what is holding you back. Think about a habit you started but later stopped. Maybe it was a morning walk or journaling before bed. What made it hard to keep going? Did the timing feel wrong? Did the habit feel forced? These questions are worth asking because the answers help you adjust instead of giving up entirely.

Reflection does not have to be complicated. It can be as simple as asking yourself three quick questions at the end of the week. What went well? What felt difficult? What would I change next week? Writing down your thoughts can make patterns easier to spot and decisions easier to make. If you notice that you keep skipping a habit, try changing when or how you approach it. An evening routine that feels rushed might work better in the morning. A habit that feels dull could become more engaging by pairing it with something enjoyable, like listening to music or drinking your favorite coffee.

Check-in with yourself during the day. Take a moment while waiting for a meeting or during a short break to review your progress. Ask yourself if you are staying focused or if something needs adjusting. Small shifts in your approach can make a big difference in how manageable habits feel. Feedback from others can also provide insights you may not have considered. A coworker might notice patterns you missed, like skipping breaks or taking on too much at once. Be open to comments and use them to spot areas where slight changes could improve your habits.

To make reflection easier, set aside some dedicated time in your schedule to review your progress. Note what was successful and what was not. Recognize trends. Did specific times of day seem more effective? Did certain habits always seem challenging to maintain? Utilize these notes to determine what to retain, modify, or eliminate. Minor adjustments frequently result in significant enhancements.

If a job seems too much to handle, divide it into smaller tasks and address them individually. If some habits are difficult to sustain, try various timings or combine them with other practices. Treat adjustments as trials, not final decisions. Test each change for a week or two and see what sticks.

Tracking your habits can keep you motivated. Use a calendar or journal to mark progress and highlight areas where adjustments helped. Adding small rewards, like a short break or a favorite snack, can also make habits feel less like chores and more like wins. In addition to weekly reflections, monthly reviews can help you see larger trends. Take some time at the end of each month to ask broader questions. Are you closer to your goals than you were four weeks ago? Which habits have made the biggest impact? Which ones need more adjustment? This process helps you stay on track and ensures that your habits evolve as your goals shift.

Consider adding visual cues to remind yourself of what works. Sticky notes on your desk, motivational quotes, or even simple symbols like checkmarks on a habit tracker can reinforce your progress. These visual reminders can keep your focus sharp and boost your motivation. Sometimes, breaking out of routine can also give you fresh insights. Try reflecting in a different space, a nice environment like a park or a quiet café. Changing your environment can make it easier to think clearly and gain new perspectives.

Finally, use reflection as a way to celebrate progress. Look back at how far you have come and recognize the effort you have put in. Rewards do not have to be big. A cup of your favorite tea or a short walk can be enough to reinforce positive behavior. Celebration reminds you that habits are not just tasks to check off but steps toward something bigger. The goal is not perfection. It is staying flexible and learning from what works and what doesn't. Regular reflection helps you keep habits useful and prevents them from turning into another source of stress. With steady adjustments and thoughtful reviews, habits stay effective and continue to support your goals.

9.3 Inspiring Those Around You to Also Focus on Healthier Ways of Working and Managing Teams

Once you begin building better habits for yourself, the next step is sharing those benefits with others. Healthy routines and mindful practices don't just improve personal well-being. They can create positive changes for entire teams. Think about how habits spread. When one person models calm, thoughtful behavior, others tend to follow. It is the same with stress management. If your team sees you setting boundaries, prioritizing tasks, and taking breaks to recharge, they are more likely to do the same.

Start by sharing what has worked for you. You do not have to give a formal speech or make a big announcement. Casual conversations can be just as effective in delivering a message. For example, you could mention how taking short breaks has improved your focus or how planning your day in small steps has made big tasks easier to handle. Invite others to try simple strategies without making it feel like a directive. You might ask, "Have you tried setting a time each day to clear your inbox? It has really helped me feel more organized." This kind of approach keeps the tone light and encourages participation rather than resistance.

Another way to inspire others is to create team habits. You could start meetings with a few deep breaths or schedule some time at the end of the week for the group to write down small wins. These shared routines not only reduce stress but also help build connections within the team. It also helps to listen. Ask your team what they struggle with most when it comes to staying organized or managing pressure. By showing interest in their challenges, you can suggest practical tips tailored to their needs. Sometimes, people just need someone to point them toward an easier way.

Recognize efforts when you see them. A simple acknowledgment like, "I noticed you took time to plan out this project. It really shows in the results," can reinforce positive changes. Small compliments build confidence and make people more willing to continue adopting better habits. If someone on your team shares a new habit that is working for them, highlight it to others. Saying, "That's a great idea! I might try that too," encourages more sharing and keeps the focus on improvement rather than criticism.

You do not have to push for perfection. The goal is to create an environment where trying new things feels safe and useful. If something doesn't work, let it go and try another approach. The point is to keep experimenting and supporting each other. Over time, these efforts can shift the culture of the team. Stressful situations will still come up, but teams that practice healthier ways of working are more likely to handle them with focus and energy instead of frustration.

When you take care of yourself and share those habits with others, you do more than manage stress. You set an example that makes healthier, more balanced workdays possible for everyone. Healthy routines and mindful practices don't just improve personal well-being. They can create positive changes for entire teams.

Final Thoughts

Building habits that keep stress away is not about perfection. It is about making small, intentional changes and being willing to adjust when needed. Whether you are focusing on consistency, reflecting on what works, or encouraging your team to do the same, the goal is progress, not perfection. Healthy habits do more than reduce stress. They create stability and make space for growth, both for you and those around you. The ideas in this chapter give you tools to build that foundation and strengthen it over time.

As we move into the final chapter, we will revisit the central question, can leaders truly be stress-free? We will explore why managing stress is more about finding balance than aiming for perfection. Leadership does not have to be defined by stress, with the right habits, it can be clear, calm, and sustainable.

10

FANTASY OR REALITY?

Stress-free leadership. The phrase itself sounds almost too good to be true. Can leaders really step into their roles, manage responsibilities, and guide teams without falling prey to stress? Or is the idea of calm, collected leadership just a comforting myth, a fantasy that fades in the face of endless deadlines and expectations? During this journey, we have looked at stress from every perspective. We have observed how it builds up slowly, sometimes in the form of ambition and resolve, and how it impacts not only the person but also entire groups. We've examined the practices, instruments, and tactics that can turn chaos into calm, one thoughtful step at a time. Yet, despite all these insights, one question persists. Is it possible for leadership to truly be stress-free?

The response isn't just a straightforward yes or no. Stress is an inherent part of life, and leadership presents its own array of difficulties. However, that doesn't imply stress must dominate. Leaders can be effective without being overwhelmed. They can be strong without burning out. And they can inspire others without sacrificing their own well-being. This chapter ties everything together.

It asks you to pause and look back, not just at the lessons learned but also at the changes you may have already started making in your own approach. It's an invitation to reflect on what balance really means to you and how you can carry these ideas forward. Leadership doesn't have to be a struggle. With the right mindset and habits, it can feel purposeful, steady and even stress-free.

Let's take one final look at this question. Is stress-free leadership a fantasy, or is it something you can truly achieve? And more importantly, what does it take to make it your reality?

10.1 Can Leaders Really Be Stress-Free?

The idea of stress-free leadership may sound ambitious, but is it truly out of reach? Leadership, by its very nature, comes with pressure. Deadlines, decisions, and expectations create an environment where stress can thrive. Yet stress is not the enemy. Instead, it is how we respond to it that makes the difference. Stress-free leadership does not mean eliminating challenges or avoiding problems. It means building the awareness and tools to face them with focus and confidence. Effective leaders recognize patterns, identify triggers early, and take deliberate steps to stay balanced. Planning ahead, prioritizing tasks, and delegating responsibilities create structure without creating overwhelm.

In earlier discussions, we looked at how stress can quietly take hold through unchecked habits and unrealistic expectations. Small adjustments, like pausing before reacting, creating intentional boundaries, and reflecting on what works, can stop stress from escalating. Leaders who set priorities, protect their time, and make room for recovery are better equipped to handle pressure without feeling overwhelmed. Reflection ensures these strategies stay relevant even when circumstances change. At its core, stress-free leadership is about preparation and adaptability. It is about knowing when to take action and when to pause. Small steps, like taking a breath before a meeting or stepping away for a short walk, keep stress from building up. Developing habits that reinforce calmness shifts the focus from reacting to responding.

This does not mean stress will disappear entirely. Challenges as a leader are unavoidable. What changes is how leaders handle those challenges. Leaders who reflect, adjust, and build supportive environments turn pressure into productivity instead of panic. Imagine starting your day with clarity instead of chaos. Imagine a team that feels supported, where collaboration flows easily, and expectations are clear. These are not distant goals. They are achievable outcomes of consistent effort and intentional habits. Leaders who establish routines that emphasize balance find that stress no longer controls their actions. Instead, it sharpens their decisions and focus.

Stress-free leadership is not about perfection. It is about being intentional, prepared, and flexible. Balance, not flawlessness, is what makes calm and effective leadership feel realistic and achievable.

10.2 Encouraging You to Take What You've Learned and Lead with Clarity and Calmness

Leadership often tests your limits. It demands decisions, accountability, and the ability to stay composed under pressure. Yet, as we've seen, leading effectively doesn't mean pushing through stress blindly. It means managing it with care, purpose, and strategy. Clarity and calmness are not traits that appear overnight. They are the results of consistent habits and intentional planning. Leaders who focus on creating systems that work for them find it easier to handle sudden challenges without losing focus. They build time for reflection, learning from both successes and missteps. These leaders understand that setbacks are not failures but lessons that refine their approach.

Calmness begins with preparation. Knowing what is ahead and having a plan reduces panic and gives you control over the situation. Whether it's organizing your day, prioritizing tasks, or setting boundaries, simple practices lay the foundation for a steadier mindset. Leaders who take time to prepare avoid the last-minute chaos that breeds unnecessary stress. Clarity grows through awareness. Leaders who stay mindful of their emotions and triggers are better at managing reactions. They understand that not every problem requires an immediate solution. Pausing to assess situations before acting allows decisions to be guided by purpose rather than panic.

Equally important is building supportive environments. Calm leaders encourage collaboration, communicate expectations clearly, and celebrate progress. They make space for team members to share challenges and ideas, creating a culture where problem-solving replaces panic. This approach doesn't just help leaders. It inspires others. Teams that work under calm, collected leadership mirror those qualities. They learn to handle pressure with focus instead of frustration. Habits and attitudes shape the culture of the entire team.

The strategies discussed earlier have shown how small, consistent steps can lead to big results. Protecting personal time, setting limits, reflecting on what works, and encouraging healthier ways of working all add up. These practices make calmness feel less like an ideal and more like a habit. Leadership isn't about eliminating stress entirely. It is about reducing its impact and building the ability to recover quickly. Calmness and clarity come from knowing what matters most and focusing energy there.

In addition to personal habits, successful leaders focus on consistency. Routine strengthens discipline and reduces the feeling of being overburdened. Building a proper work schedule and planning accordingly, whether through morning planning sessions, end-of-day reflections, or weekly check-ins, helps leaders create order within uncertainty. The more predictable their process, the easier it is to handle the unexpected. Resilient leaders also embrace flexibility. While structure creates stability, adaptability prevents rigidity. They know when to stick to the plan and when to adjust. This balance of discipline and flexibility creates a steady foundation without affecting creativity or growth.

Equally important is self-awareness. Leaders who regularly evaluate their emotional state and energy levels are better at catching signs of burnout before it escalates. They set boundaries and prioritize recovery time, understanding that breaks are not setbacks but essential for sustainability. Finally, calmness is reinforced by focusing on purpose.

Leaders who remind themselves why they lead find it easier to stay grounded. Purpose acts as an anchor during stressful moments, turning obstacles into opportunities to reinforce values and inspire confidence.

So, take what you've learned and make it your foundation. Start each day with purpose. Approach problems with perspective. Trust the habits you've built to keep you grounded. Stress-free leadership may not mean the absence of challenges, but it does mean facing them with focus, strength, and a sense of direction.

10.3 Is Stress-Free Leadership Just a Fantasy? Can It Really Be Achieved?

Is stress-free leadership just a fantasy? Or can it truly become a reality? This question has guided every page of this book. The answer is not about eliminating stress completely but learning to manage it in ways that create clarity, calmness, and growth. Think about how far we have come. We began by confronting the reality of stress and how it seeps into routines, affects decisions, and spreads through teams. But we also uncovered the tools to counterbalance that stress. We looked at simple habits that restore stability, boundaries that protect energy, and reflections that sharpen focus. We saw how preparation, organization, and awareness create a foundation for steady and purposeful leadership.

It may feel like stress-free leadership is out of reach when deadlines pile up, and responsibilities stretch you thin. But reality proves otherwise. Leadership that keeps stress under control is achievable through small, intentional steps that build resilience and reinforce balance. Stress-free leadership does not require perfection. It is built on progress. It is about pausing before reacting, focusing on priorities, and recognizing when to adjust. Leaders who prepare, plan, and act with purpose shape their reality rather than letting stress shape them.

This book has shown that stress does not have to be the enemy. It can motivate and guide when handled with the right mindset. Leaders who reflect, adjust, and stay consistent turn stress into fuel for focus and growth. Stress-free leadership is not about avoiding pressure. It is about responding to it with clarity, balance, and intention. It is about transforming challenges into opportunities to lead with strength and purpose.

As you close this book and return to your role, ask yourself one final question. Will you let stress define your leadership, or will you define your reality? The choice is yours. Stress-free leadership is not a dream. It is a reality that begins with preparation, consistency, and intentional habits. The strategies and tools you have explored in these chapters are now yours to use. The foundation is in place, and the next steps are yours to take.

AFTERWORD

When you think of leadership, what comes to mind? Is it long hours, endless decisions, and constant demands? Or is it the ability to guide others with calmness, focus, and strength? The question that has been repeated throughout this book remains, can leadership truly be stress-free?

This book has not promised perfection, nor has it suggested that challenges will disappear. What it has done is show that stress-free leadership is not a distant fantasy but a reality built through thoughtful habits, clear boundaries, and intentional actions. It has demonstrated that leading with clarity and calmness does not require eliminating pressure but learning to manage it with purpose. We started by acknowledging the realities of stress and its impact on both leaders and teams. We then moved through strategies for recognizing triggers, strengthening resilience, and building habits that turn stress into focus rather than fear. Each chapter layered practical tools and techniques that leaders can use to stay grounded, even when challenges arise.

You learned how small, consistent actions create big changes. From protecting personal time and prioritizing tasks to reflecting on what works and inspiring teams, the lessons in this book focused on building systems that keep stress at bay. These systems do not rely on quick fixes but instead encourage progress, adaptability, and growth. As you reflect on this journey, remember that leadership is not defined by the absence of stress but by how you respond to it. Leaders who plan ahead, set boundaries, and lead by example are not immune to stress. They are equipped to handle it without losing their balance.

The final takeaway is this, stress-free leadership is not a fantasy. It is a process. It requires effort, awareness, and persistence, but it is achievable. It is about building habits that keep stress manageable, creating space for reflection, and being intentional about how you lead. So what comes next? You have the tools. You have the mindset. You have the strategies. What you do with them will shape the kind of leader you become. Let this book be the foundation, and let your actions build the results. Lead well. Lead intentionally. Lead stress-free.

9 798889 777649 8